AF324654

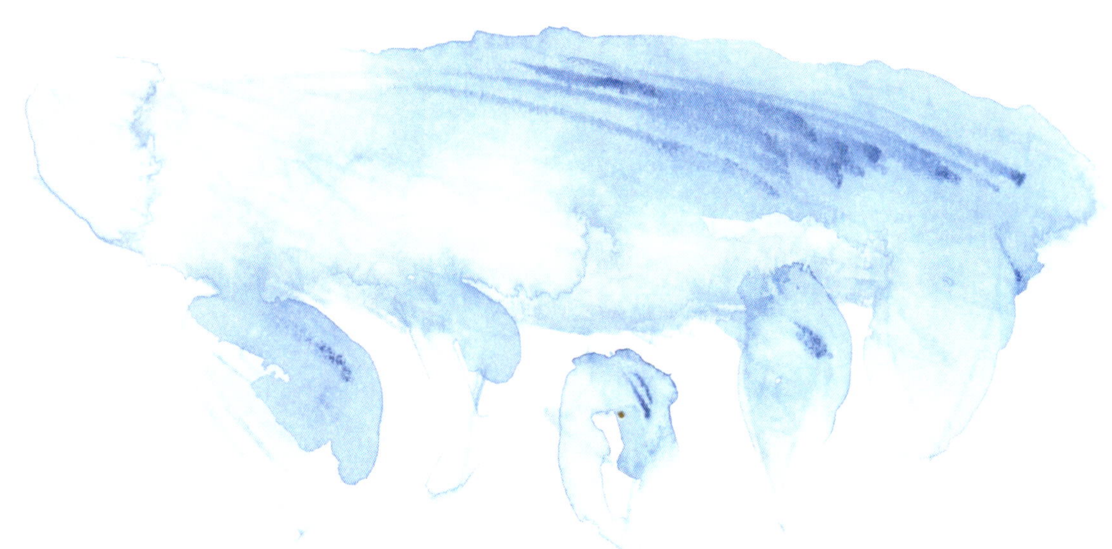

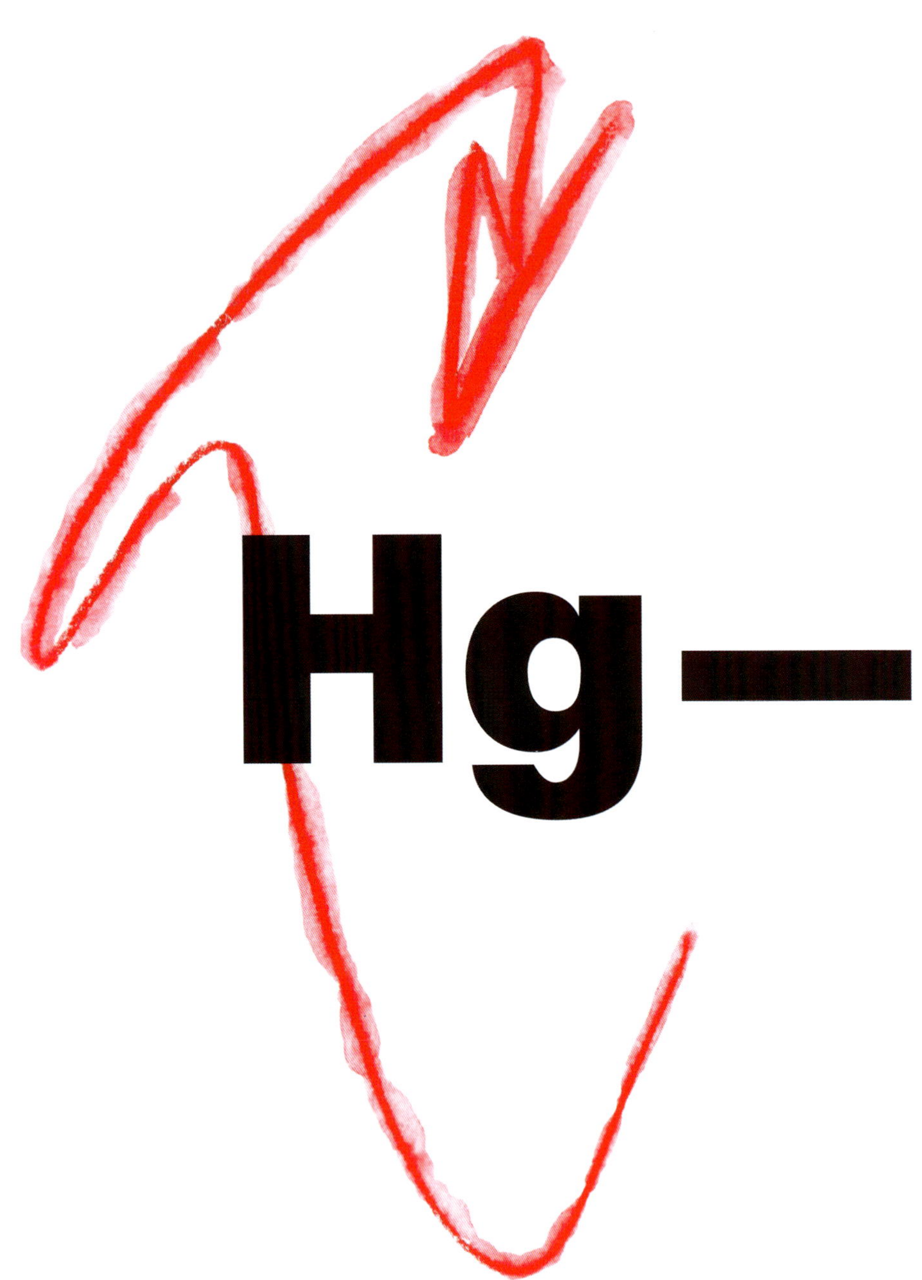
Hg —

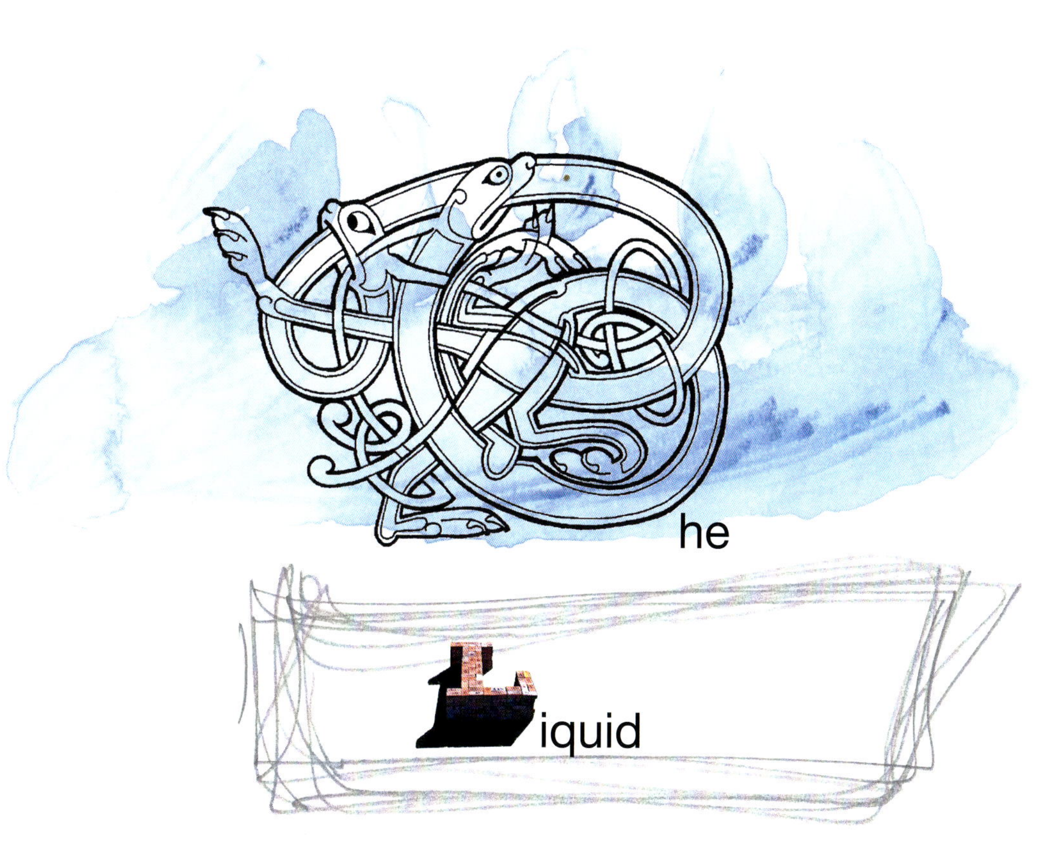

he

Liquid

Hg—The Liquid

Ward Tietz

1913 Press

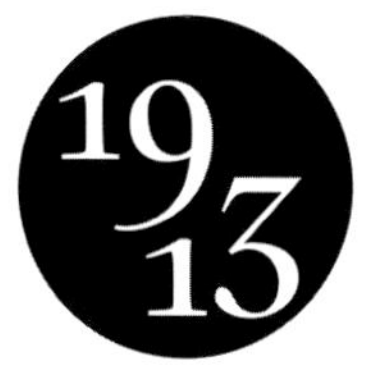

Hg—The Liquid
Copyright © 2019 by Ward Tietz

1913 Press
www.1913press.org
1913press@gmail.com

1913 is a not-for-profit collective. Contributions to 1913 Press may be tax-deductible.

Manufactured in the oldest country in the world, The United States of America.

Many thanks to all the artists, from this century and the last, who made this project possible.

Founder & Editrice: Sandra Doller
Vice-Editor: Ben Doller
Cover Design: Anne C. Kerns, Anne Likes Red, Inc.
Cover Photos: Thinkstock Photo; Ward Tietz
Book Design: Anne C. Kerns, Anne Likes Red, Inc.

ISBN: 978-0-9779351-6-1

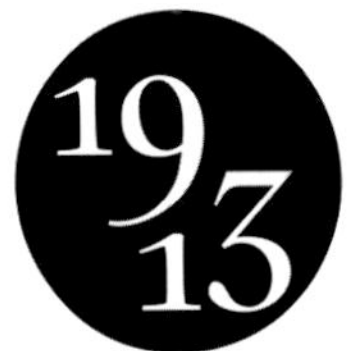

For Lydia

Contents

Preface

UP AS ITS CHIMERA: A PREFACE

Loosely, this book functions like an illuminated manuscript. I designed the letter images found on the following pages to function like rubrics, or *enluminures*, to use the French word, to anchor and illuminate both word and page. All of the rubric letters in this manuscript, except the twin-lioness "T" taken from Aidan Meehan's *Celtic Design: Illuminated Letters* on the title page, come from photographs of letter and word objects that I designed or built in the 1980s and 90s and were part of temporary installations in public parks or were used in performances.

If they are rubrical, what do they illuminate? The larger text on the pages that follow, I'm presuming, but also the semiotic and temporal gap that exists between what the text is—what it initiates in reading and viewing—and what and where it comes from: how a text is not its writing.

A text is "a form of artificial memory…created by the reduction of speech sounds to space" (Calinescu 27) and though we usually never know—or even care—how the duration, rhythm and memory of writing a text compare with those of a final textual reading, we have a sense of an ideal differential through the analog of speech. In speech, the duration and rhythm of speaking equal the duration and rhythm of hearing, and while the writing and reading of a text only rarely approach this ideal, we read as if it were readily achievable, as if reading a text were rhythmically and existentially comparable to its writing.

The *enluminures*, the rubrics, then, demonstrate a radical difference between a writing and its text and break the presumption of rhythmic and existential equivalence. As objects, and then as images, many of the rubric letters took days, even weeks, to write. Lugubrious in their writing, rubrics fall out of the rhythmic suspension of language and its basis in sound. They maintain no real connection to "inner speech" (Vygotsky), or to the temporal unity of Saussure's "sound image," which are writing's witness—in reading, of language—in mind. Instead, rubrical writing produces individual letters, slowly, one after the next. Mute, they are uncoupled from the writer's thought as represented in words or phrases. Through this divestment of sound, our percepts shift in reaction, away from reading, toward viewing and an emphasis on action and objects.

The rubrical letters and the words that they are attached to are different in what they do and how they mean. By emphasizing the different existential/temporal nature of rubrical letters, I hope to connect the non-rubrical text, through imbrication, more emphatically, to a larger world of objects and deeds. Such a connection is aided by the way the rubrics work against their text, rhythmically, effectively resisting the textual world they inhabit, defaulting back—harkening back—as images, to the world of objects and actions that preceded them.

Word-images function as both icons and symbols; they oscillate semiotically. By "icon" and "symbol," I refer to two of the terms of the standard triadic, semiotic typology of C.S. Peirce. Peirce's sign categories of index, icon and symbol track rising degrees of conventionality and arbitrariness. They are useful here not in the strict taxonomic sense (I'm not interested in classification, as such), but in their ability to highlight certain aspects of the letters and words as signs and to show how context, contiguity and rhythm affect the construal of these aspects. The example of a footprint as an indexical sign of someone having walked an area before us does not rely on cultural convention for us to construe meaning. The index, then, is seen as a more natural, or "motivated," sign, and it depends on very specific spatial and temporal patterns for its motivation. The symbol, which relies almost exclusively on cultural convention, is at the other extreme. Words, in most cases, function symbolically: words signify or mean what they do because of the cultural conventions of usage, not because of any natural link between words themselves and their meanings. Icons are somewhere in between. They bear some similarity to what they signify, in shape, color, material, etc. Pictures or images are the most obvious icons, but sight does not have any privilege to the category. An artificial flavor would be an icon of the represented flavor.

The illumination of the text, through the imbrication of rubrics, promotes aspects of similarity between the text—what it is—and what it signifies. To use Peirce's terminology, illumination shifts the text's sign structure—away from the arbitrariness of the symbol and the remove and "thirdness" of textual representation, past "secondness" and its betweenness and mediation, toward an ideal "firstness" of the full icon, where writing cannot sustain a text, where semiosis must ultimately fail and dissolve back into a brute state of objects and materials.

Firstness for Peirce "is the mode of being of that which is such as it is, positively and without reference to anything else" (8.328). The rubrics attempt to achieve this through their objectification. Iconicity is "a matter of degree" since "a sign is iconic to the extent to which it itself has the properties of its denotata" (Morris 191). The complete icon, where sign resembles its object in every aspect, is no longer a sign, but a thing in its raw firstness—a sign that signifies nothing, but itself.

I won't pretend that *Hg—The Liquid* achieves anything like a raw firstness, but the "matter of degree" of the icon and a rubrical writing that works against the symbolical functioning of its text establish a dream state of firstness for the larger text that the rubrics inhabit; it offers the rubric letter up as its chimera. The individual word-image, where a rubric is folded into a word, is the microcosm of this same state, and while it is a state or condition, it is also a multiplicity. Like a Necker cube, which can be seen as either convex or concave, such a multiplicity cannot usually be experienced simultaneously. A word-image is construed as a word (read) or an image (viewed), never both at the same time. The oscillation between the poles of word (symbol) and image (icon) participate in a meta-cognitive moment, a sense that any given moment

exists comparatively—since one state must precede and the other follow—or maybe
even interchangeably: a before could have been an after, an after, a before.

PRIOR EXISTENCE (OUTSIDE THE TEXT)

I said that the *enluminures*, the rubric letters, illuminate the semiotic and temporal
gap that exists between the text and its writing. Much of this gap is addressed by
iconization of the text, but at a more specific level, the rubrics—as images—also
speak to shifts in materiality. This shift is not reflected in the actual materiality of the
text; rather, it is thematized in the rubric image (what they show and signify in an ontic
state: wax letters, brick letters, etc.) and the information contained in the concordance
as to the letters' original weight and size. These make up the text's precondition.
The material, size, weight, and the larger three-dimensional word-objects that the
enluminures were extracted from, what I call the lexemes, are listed alphabetically in
the concordance that follows. Lexemes are usually considered to be minimal units
or base forms of language. Here, I stress the base—its firstness in material and
implicit hylomorphism: matter as first cause—and its thirdness as a textual fragment
representing language generally.

For example, the   the   the   and the   are
the "c," the "o," the "a," and the "x" that made the floating (in water) wax word "coax."
"Coax," the verb, is the lexeme for all of these rubric letters; it is their semantic, lexical
genesis, the *enluminures* its residue. You might want to challenge such a notion at this
point. Why lexeme? Why residue? Such things wouldn't be present or palpable in the
text if I didn't insist on them. I admit that if there is a lexical or material or iconic residue,
it doesn't stick. The text cleans up; it carries everything away through its symbolization;
it forgets its origins.

"To write is to have the passion of the origin" (Derrida 295), but which origin? The text will
never tell all, but the rubric, in its iconic and indexical polysemy, can show, in part. The
rubric can show an origin, even if it came after a text that it illuminates. But I am not
speaking here so much as an author with designs on meanings as I am as a witness.
I'm giving information for what it's worth. I could be silent, or I could tell, even if I don't
tell everything. These installation words, the lexemes, are where the rubric letters came
from, but they don't appear in the text itself. To that extent they are hidden much as
every text must hide the circumstances and true materials of its writing.

So, the 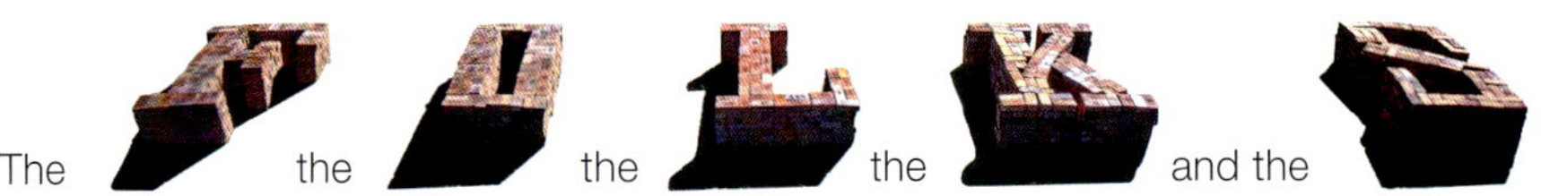 the the and the
are the "h," the "n," the "e," the "y" that made the floating (in pond water) wax word
"honey." "Honey" is the lexeme for all of these letters (even as its "o" is absent as rubric).
Wax floats, so did "honey." Each letter functioned as a candle that was lit at night.

The the the the and the
are the "F," the "O" (brick), the "L," the "K," and the "S" that made the flat-standing
word "FOLKS." "FOLKS" is their lexeme; in its abstraction it's absent the original
FOLKS' five tons.

The was the first and last letter in the upright-floating word "glug." The rubric, as
an image, is cut-off, as its descender extended below the base (water) line.

The the and the are the "k," the "i" and the "t" of a concrete
(literally) "kite." The "e" is missing; there was no good photograph of it, so making a
rubric of it became impossible.

The has no lexeme. Designed as a performative rubric, it has primarily been
used in poetic performances, first in the Geneva Festival in *Accompong.*

The is an "O" of an "OX." Chest-high, it was made of ice and a hug (X) and a
kiss (O). The "X" marks the spot of its missing ice rubric in the concordance and text;
this spot is taken up by the wax "x" of "coax."

The   occurred first in "SAVE," as in "SAVE mon(k)ey." "SAVE monkey" was the
word-object installation's title (along with a large capital A in the middle, so it read,
more readily, as "SAVE A monkey"); as part of an exhibition in Empire-Fulton Ferry
State Park, these letters and words stood in the shadow of the Brooklyn Bridge until
the Coast Guard classified them an "attractive nuisance."

The lexemes lead and the *enluminures*, the rubrics, follow; this is the way it is, but not
was. Who knows what anything should, or could be? Here is a could, a should: the
larger qualities of the text should flow, like the title, like mercury, like *Hg—The Liquid*.

Hg—The Liquid: (atomic radius: A 1.76)
                 (atomic weight: u 200.59)
                 (atomic density: g/mL 13.53).

Concordance

LETTER	MATERIAL	SIZE	WEIGHT	LEXEME
	wax	3" x 2.5' x 2.5'	15 lbs.	"coax"
	wax	3" x 2.5' x 2.5'	15 lbs.	"coax"
	wax	3" x 2.5' x 2.5'	15 lbs.	"honey"
	brick	2.5' x 3.5' x 5'	2,000 lbs.	"FOLKS"
	styrofoam	3' x 2' x 3"	15 lbs.	"glug"
	wax	3" x 2.5" x 3'	20 lbs.	"honey"
	concrete	2' x 1.5' x 3"	15 lbs.	"kite"
	brick	2.5' x 3.5' x 5'	2,000 lbs.	"FOLKS"
	concrete	3' x 3' x 3"	30 lbs.	"kite"
	brick	2.5' x 3.5' x 5'	2,000 lbs.	"FOLKS"

LETTER	MATERIAL	SIZE	WEIGHT	LEXEME
	steel	3' x 3' x 1'	80 lbs.	none
	wax	3" x 2.5' x 2.5'	15 lbs.	"honey"
	ice	4' x 2' x 6"	90 lbs.	"OX"
	brick	2.5' x 3.5' x 5'	2,000 lbs.	"FOLKS"
	wax	2.5' x 2.5' x 3"	15 lbs.	"coax"
	brick	2.5' x 3.5' x 5'	2,000 lbs.	"FOLKS"
	concrete	3' x 1.5' x 3"	20 lbs.	"kite"
	wood	3' x 1.5' x 5"	20 lbs.	"SAVE"
	wax	3" x 2.5' x 2.5'	15 lbs.	"coax"
	wax	3" x 2.5' x 3.5'	20 lbs.	"honey"

Stamp of the Champignons

Stamp of the Champignons

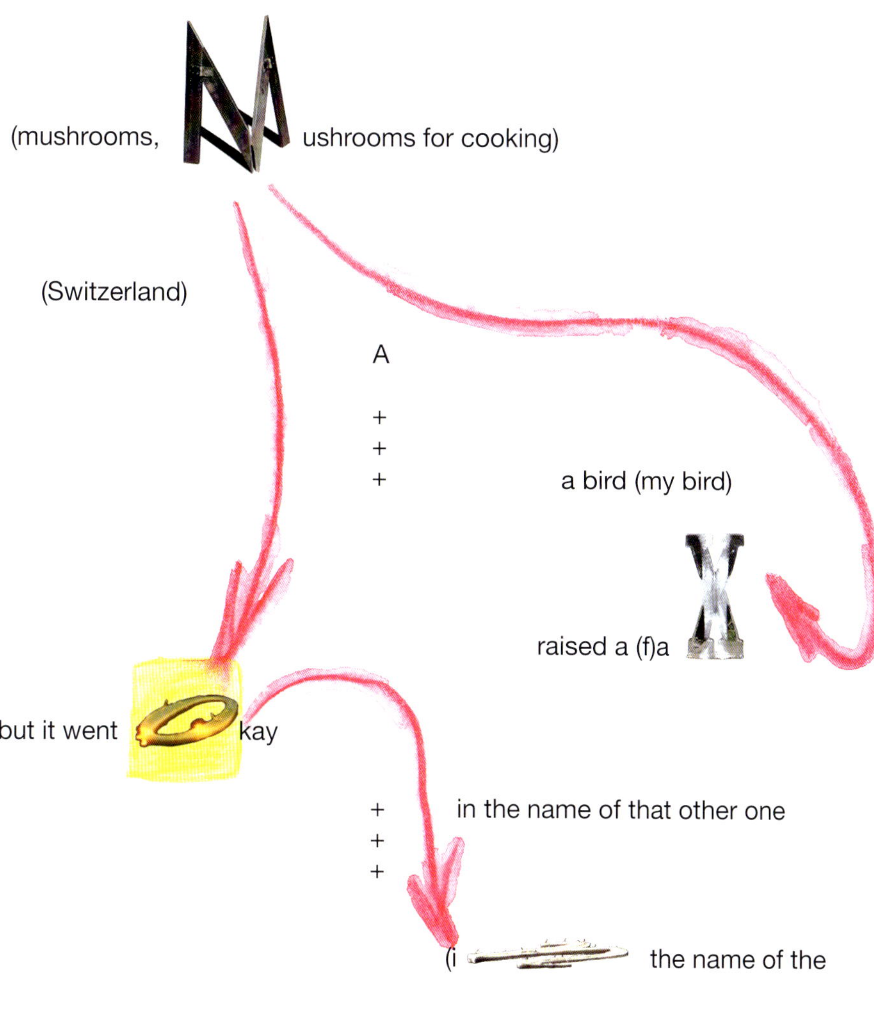

(mushrooms, mushrooms for cooking)

(Switzerland)

A

+
+
+

a bird (my bird)

raised a (f)a

but it went okay

+
+
+

in the name of that other one

(i the name of the

whole farm!)

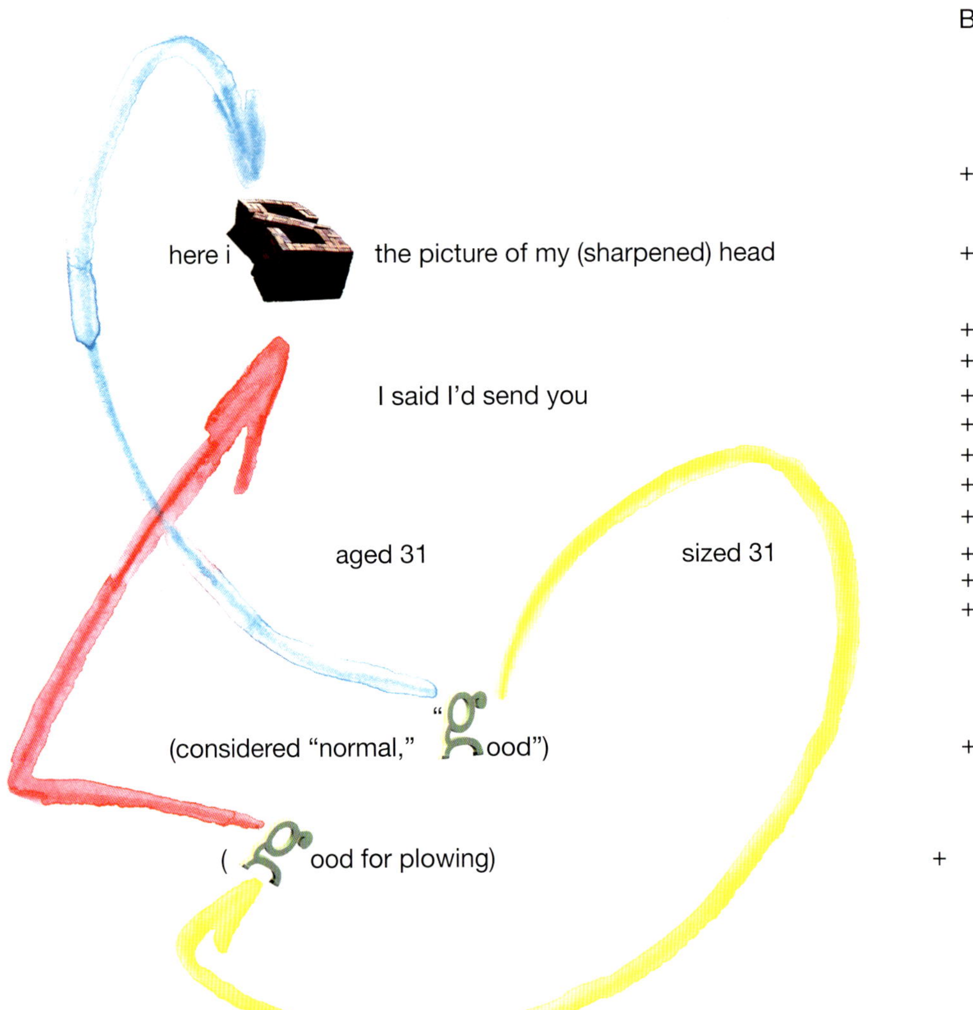
here i   the picture of my (sharpened) head

I said I'd send you

aged 31   sized 31

(considered "normal,"   "good")

(ood for plowing)

+
+
+
+
+
+
+
+
+
+

+

+

the weather we have

could 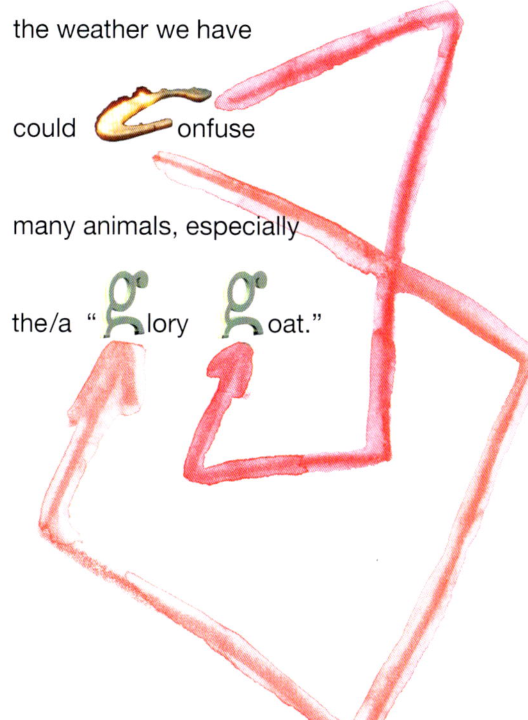onfuse

many animals, especially

the/a " lory oat."

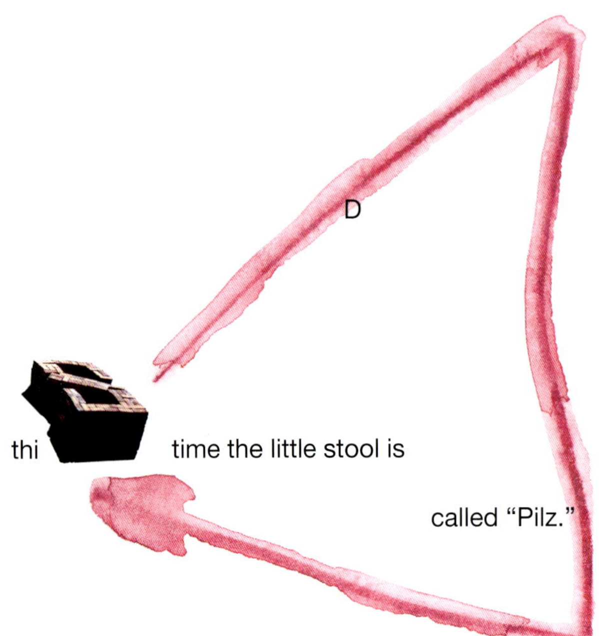

D

thi time the little stool is

called "Pilz."

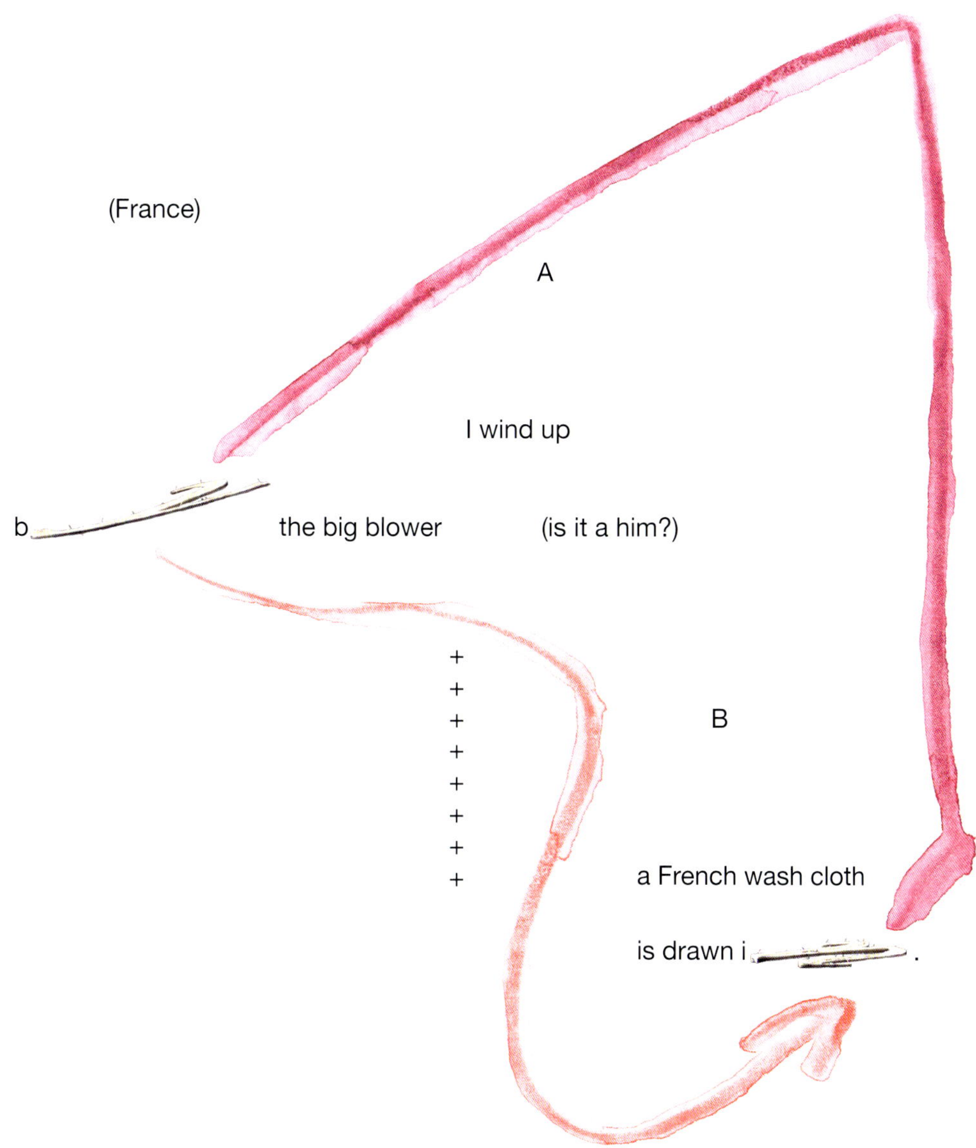

(France)

A

I wind up

b

the big blower

(is it a him?)

+
+
+
+
+
+
+
+

B

a French wash cloth

is drawn i   .

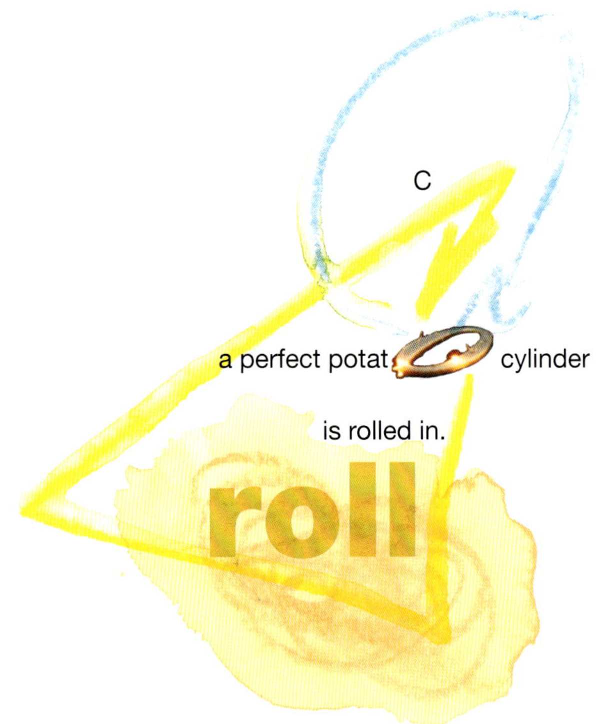

C
a perfect potat   cylinder
is rolled in.
roll

Mining Town: An Ant Family

Have you seen the mining town that used to whac   me?

+++++++++++++++++++++++++++
++++++ (Port Carbon, PA) ++++++
+++++++++++++++++++++++++++

yes

I have!

(paetcheguaho!) (yes!)

It turned m   into a fryer.

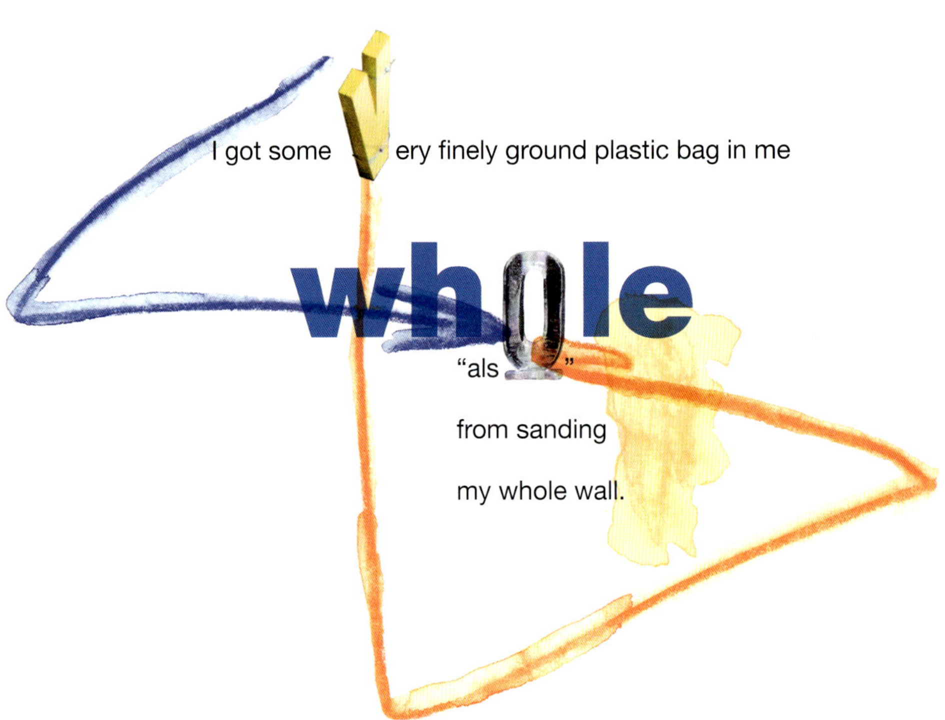

I got some very finely ground plastic bag in me

whole

"als o"

from sanding

my whole wall.

”)

This gash on my knee divides a foreign-country lower

le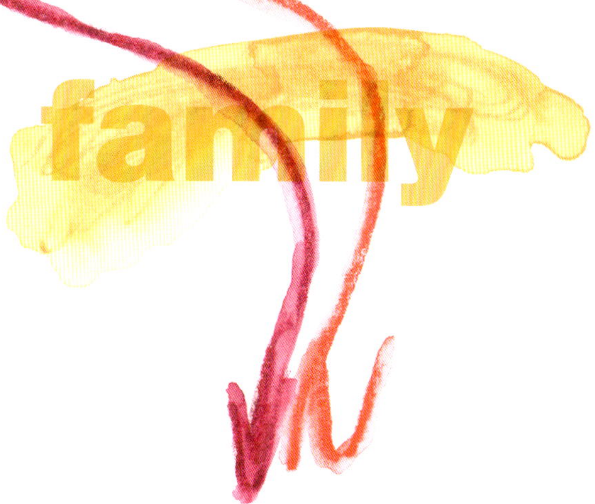 from a "state" le

You and your family cover the "state"

poles of the *pays*[1]   with a flat, hat-cover plastic.

family

---

[1] "pay-ee," (F countr   ) (France).

(I am thinking of a friend)

In one of the BeNeLux countrie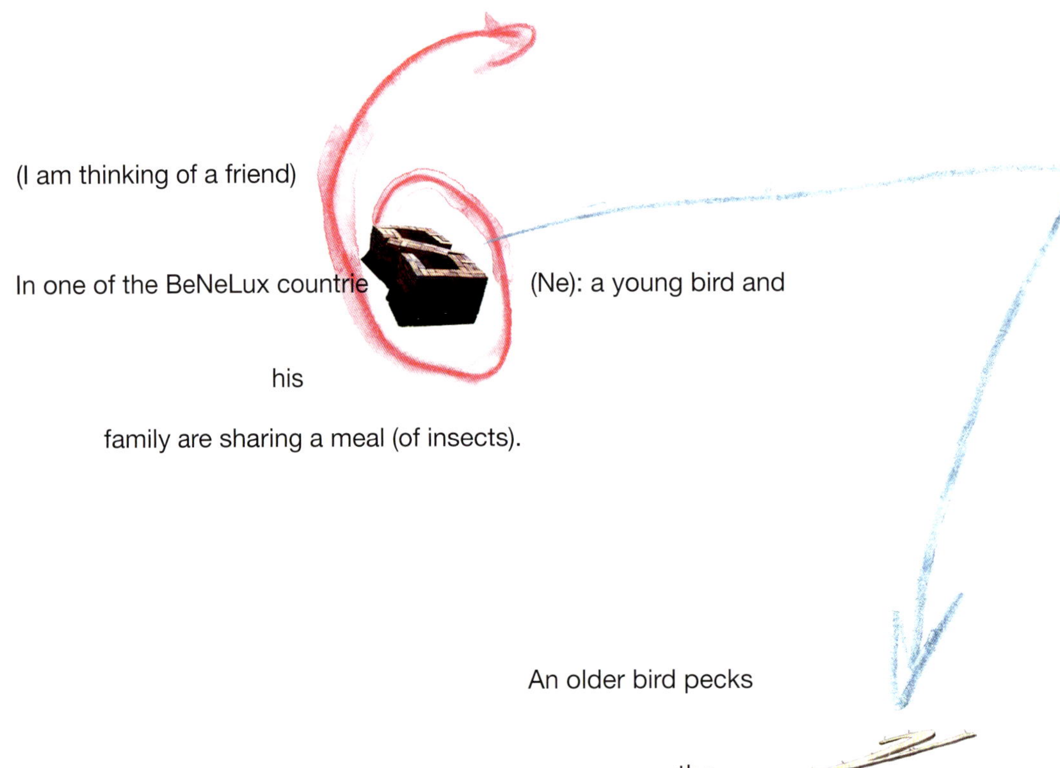(Ne): a young bird and

his

family are sharing a meal (of insects).

An older bird pecks

the

ounger bird under the eye and leaves a scar-feather.

My family and the/an ant family 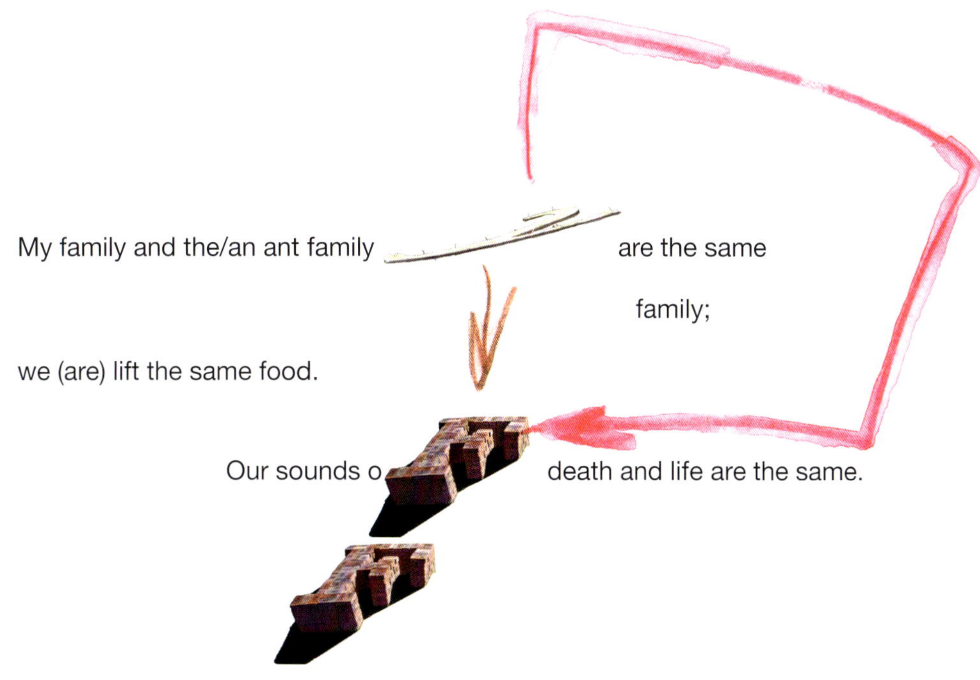 are the same

family;

we (are) lift the same food.

Our sounds o death and life are the same.

When my grandson, who is now a grown man,

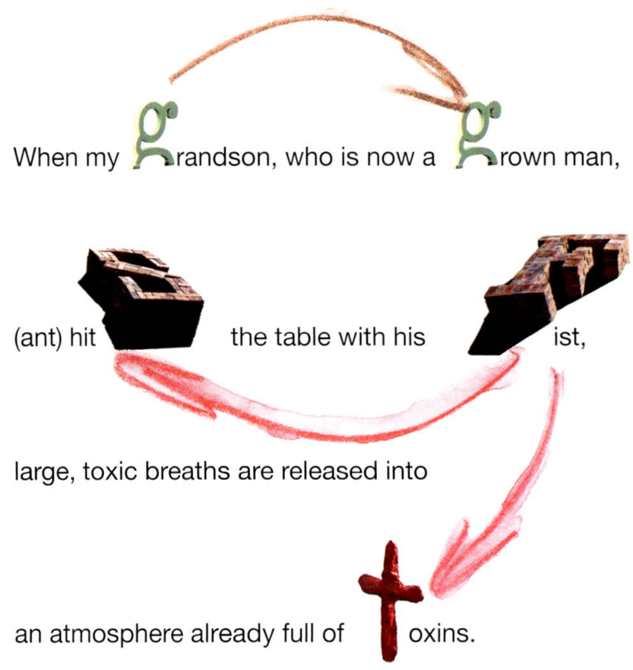

(ant) hit   the table with his   ist,

large, toxic breaths are released into

an atmosphere already full of   oxins.

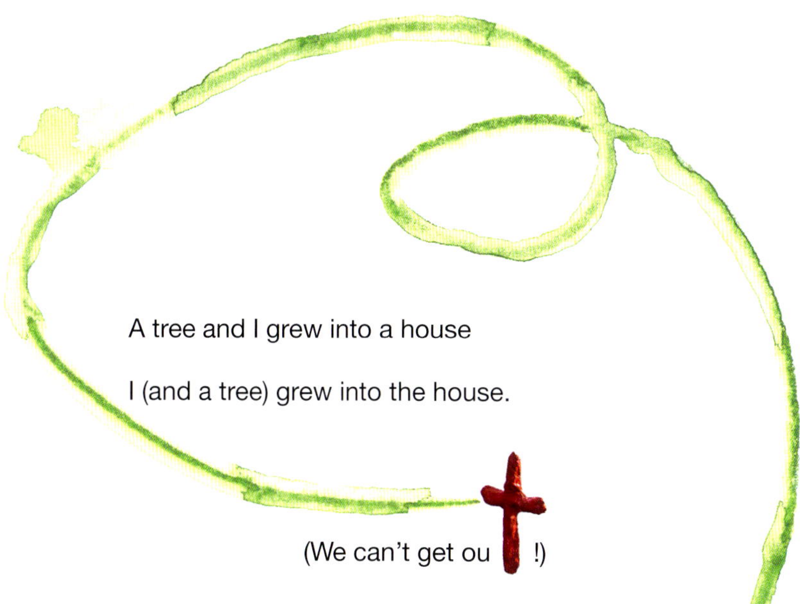

A tree and I grew into a house

I (and a tree) grew into the house.

(We can't get out !)

Under the asphalt set, really only slept, next to a seed

"semence de gazon," common grass seed;

after three decades, on March 5, 1972,

we broke through.

One, Two, I Learned from Apollo 10

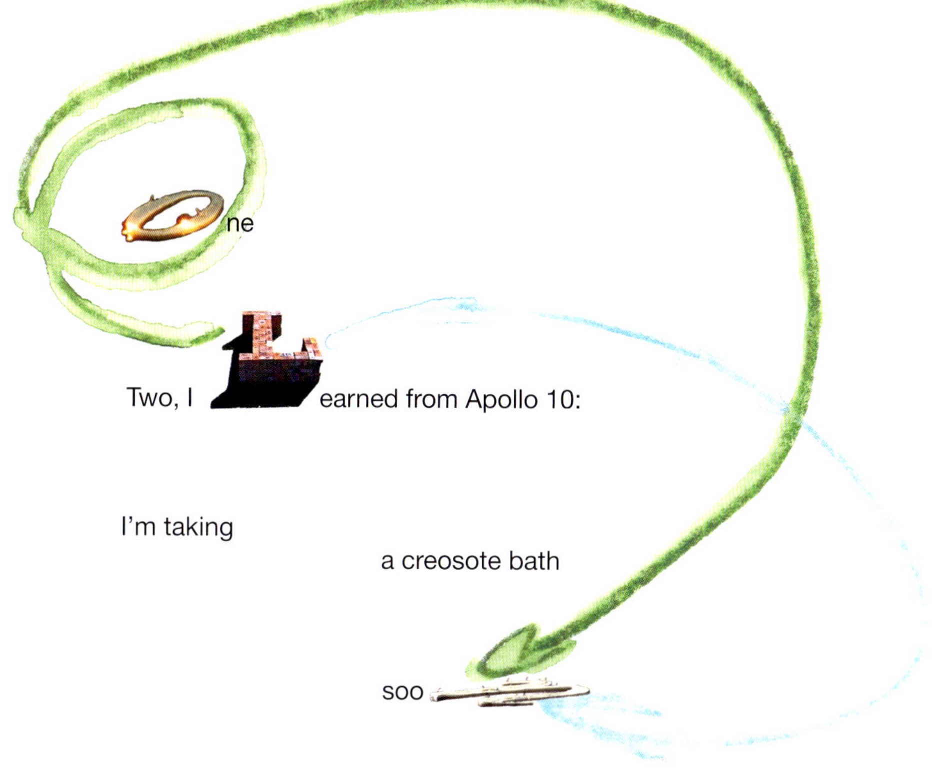

One

Two, I Learned from Apollo 10:

I'm taking

a creosote bath

soo

I realize

it's the wrong thing

and they stop it.

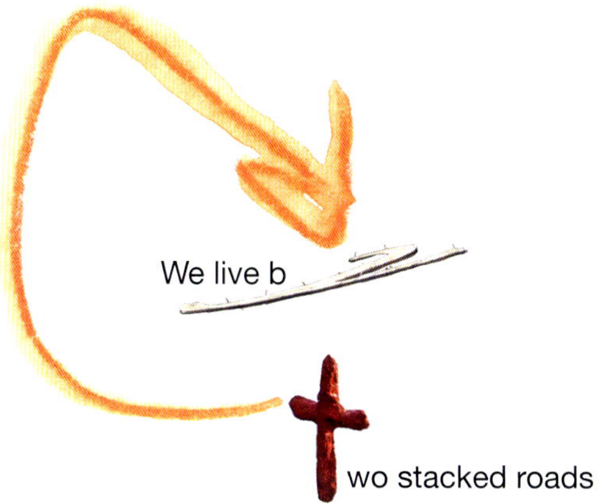

wo stacked roads

one for (eggs), one against (eggs).

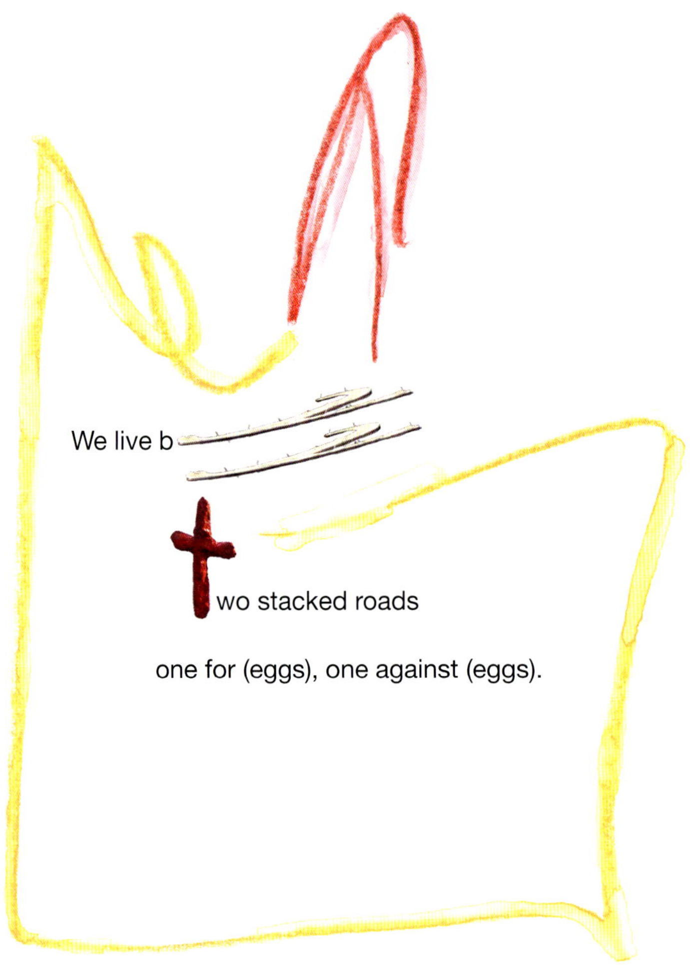

We live b
wo stacked roads
one for (eggs), one against (eggs).

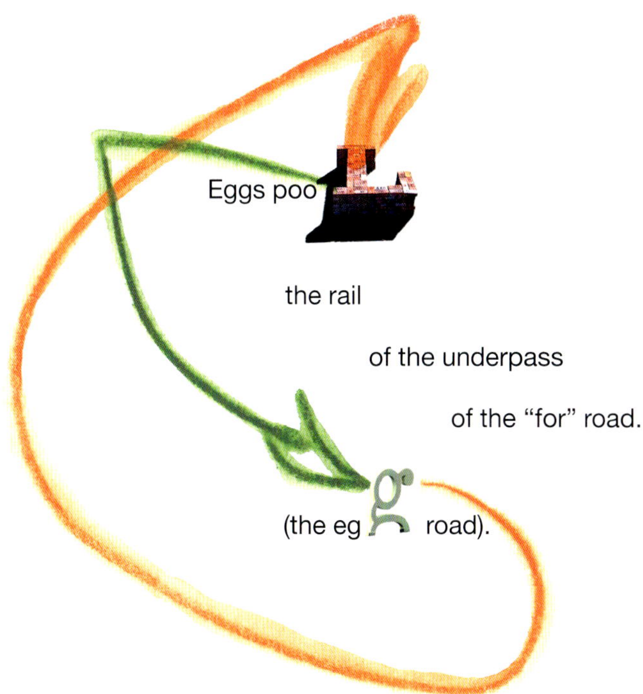

Eggs poo

the rail

of the underpass

of the "for" road.

(the eg   road).

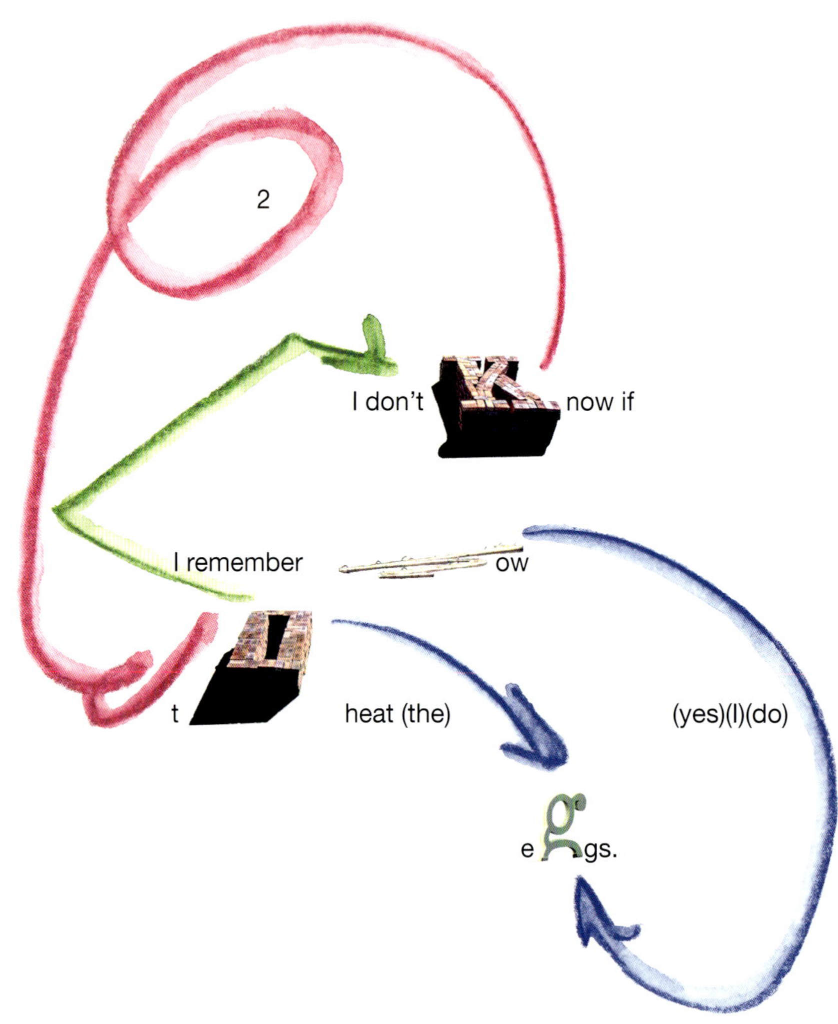

2
I don't now if
I remember ow
t heat (the) (yes)(I)(do)
e g gs.

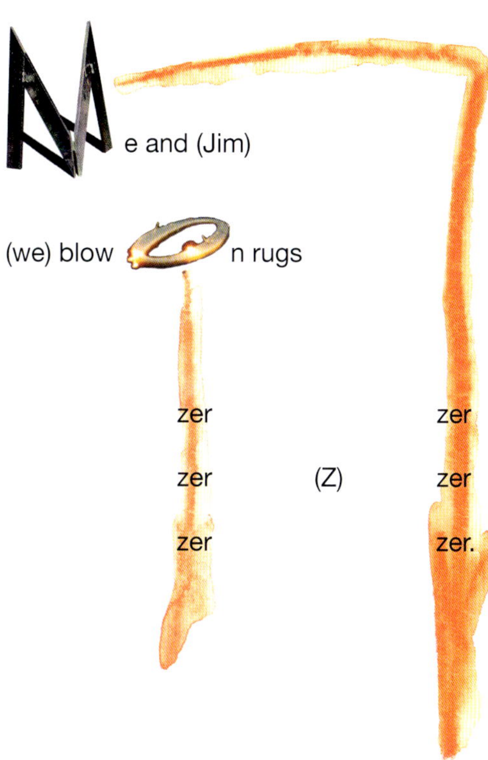
e and (Jim)
(we) blow   n rugs
zer   zer
zer   (Z)   zer
zer   zer.

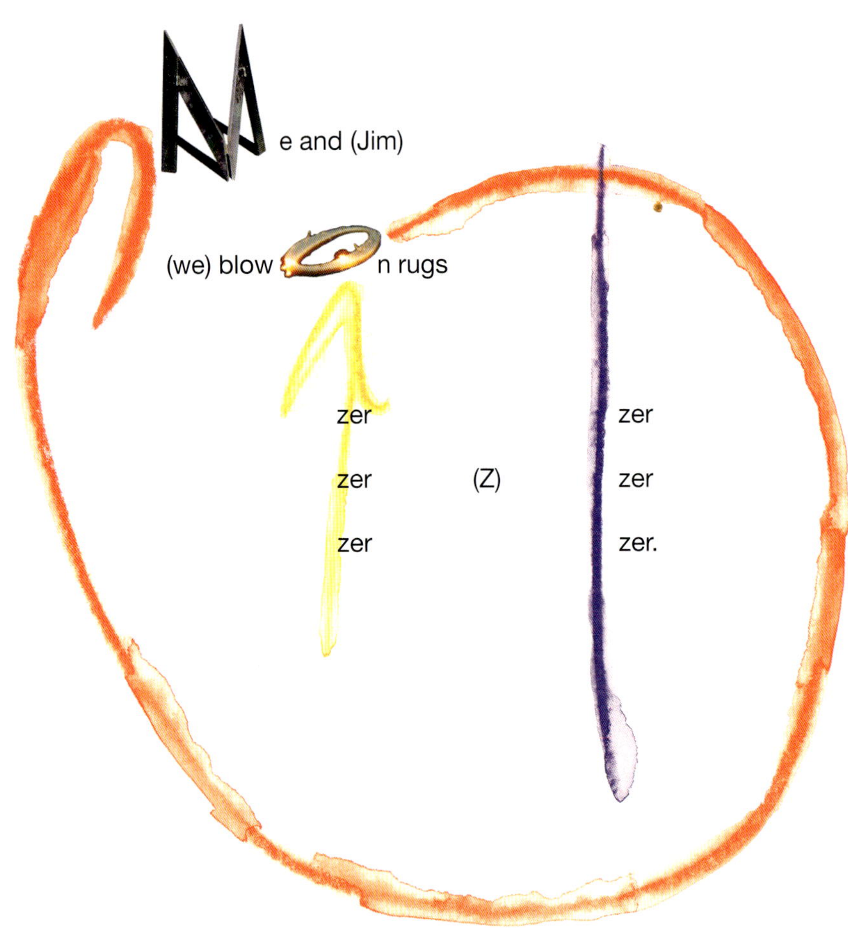
e and (Jim)
(we) blow n rugs
zer
zer
zer
(Z)
zer
zer
zer.

Boat-Slip, Little Shoe

"G _ _ _"

I was not the right person to sit on the boat roof.

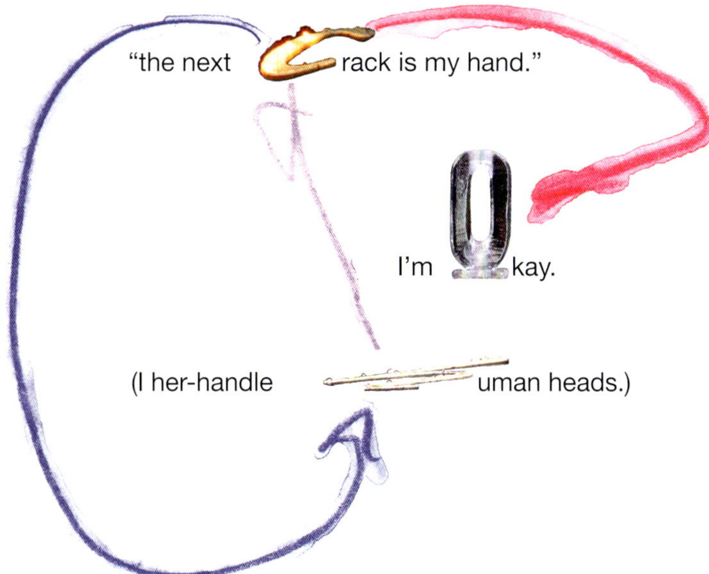

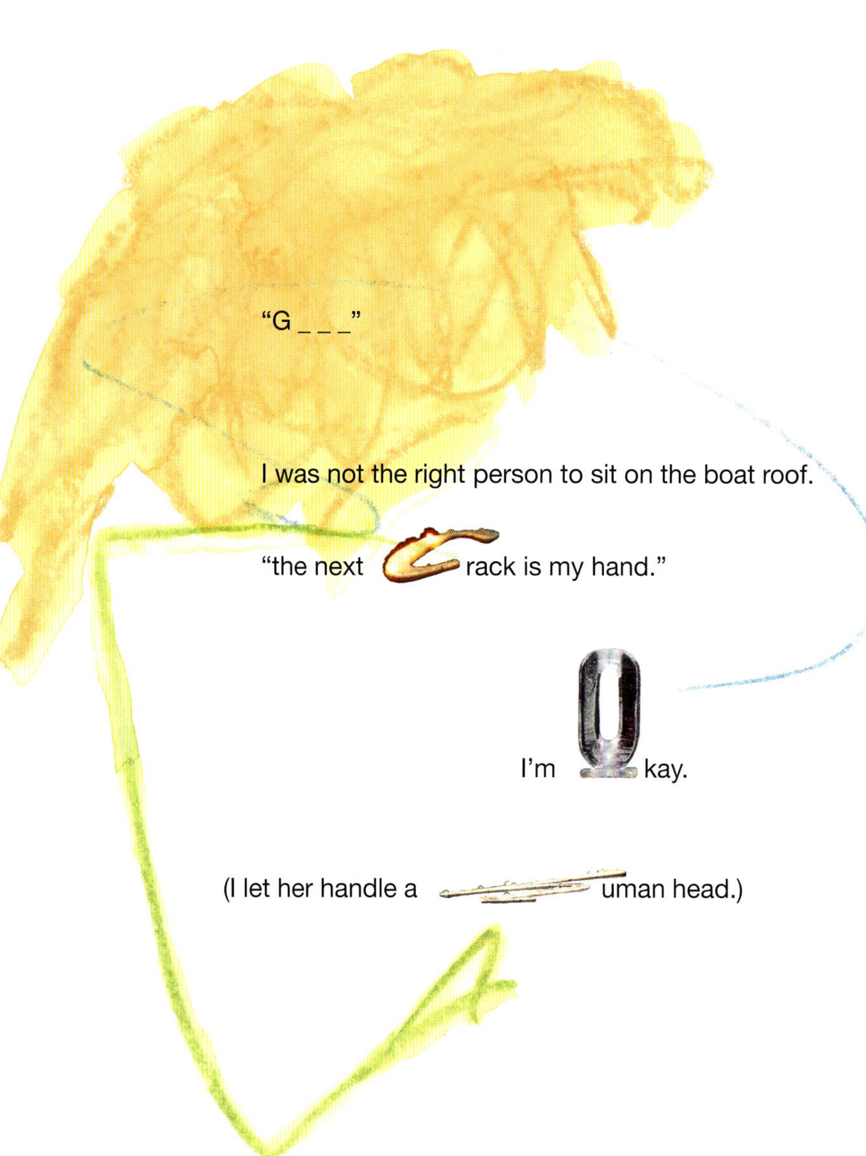

"G _ _ _"

I was not the right person to sit on the boat roof.

"the next rack is my hand."

I'm kay.

(I let her handle a uman head.)

2

W(h)ere in the boat-world are you, is your boat?

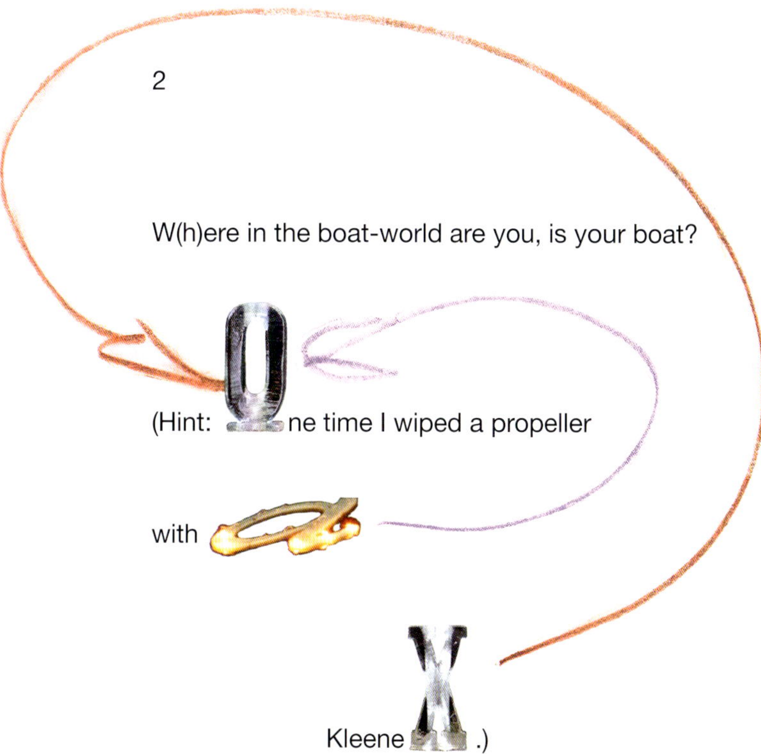

(Hint: One time I wiped a propeller

with

Kleene .)

2

W(h)ere in the boat-world are (were) you, (was) is your boat?

(Hint: One time I wiped a propeller

with

Kleene .)

3

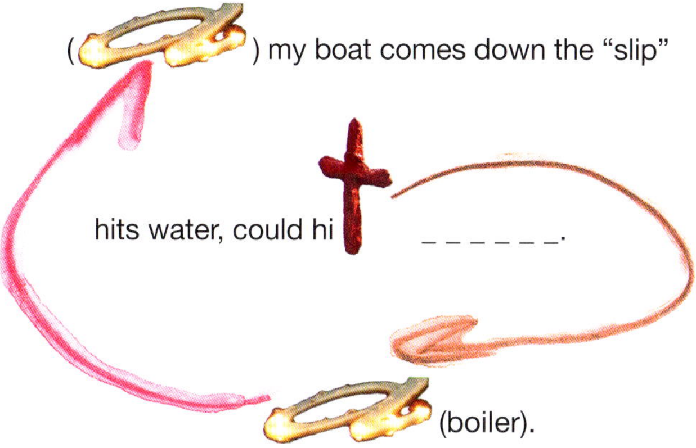

4

m   hair (pops)

(my)

wild wart (pop 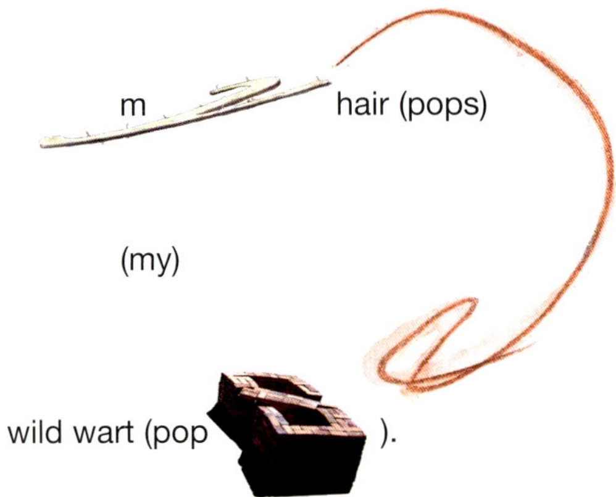).

5

sinc 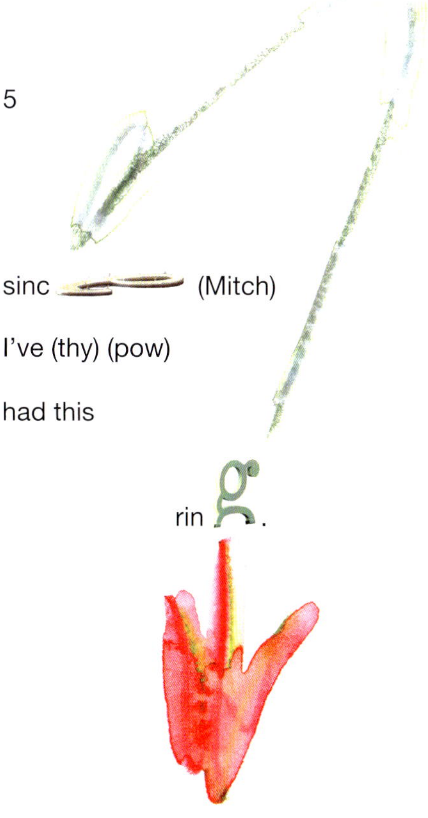 (Mitch)

I've (thy) (pow)

had this

rin g.

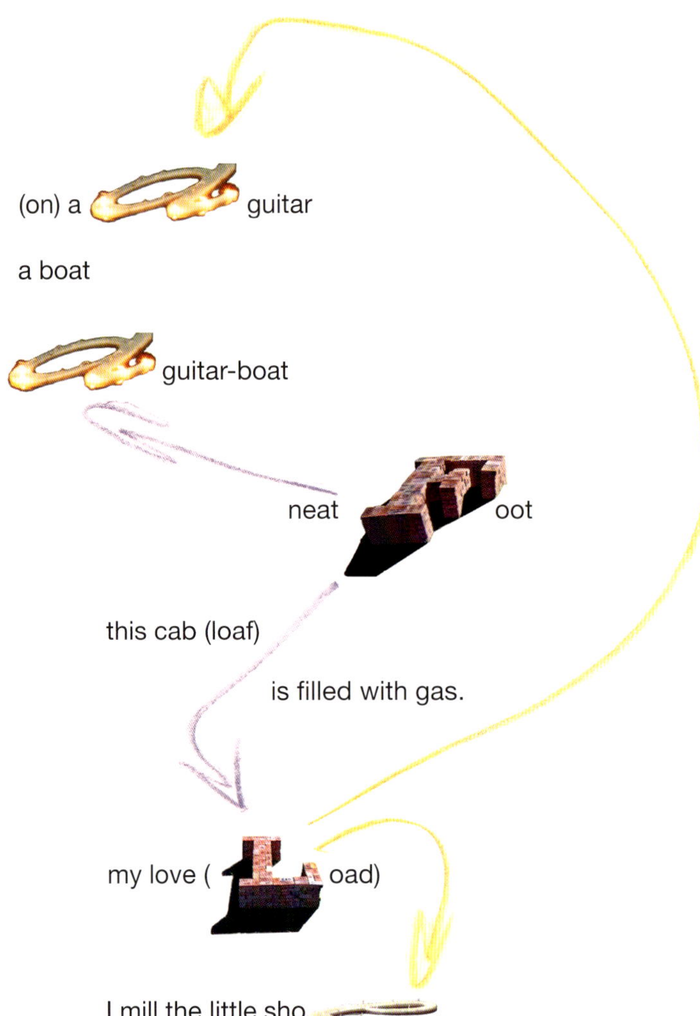

(on) a guitar

a boat

guitar-boat

neat   oot

this cab (loaf)

is filled with gas.

my love (oad)

I mill the little sho   .

A Call-In Show

I have a call-in show (7–9)

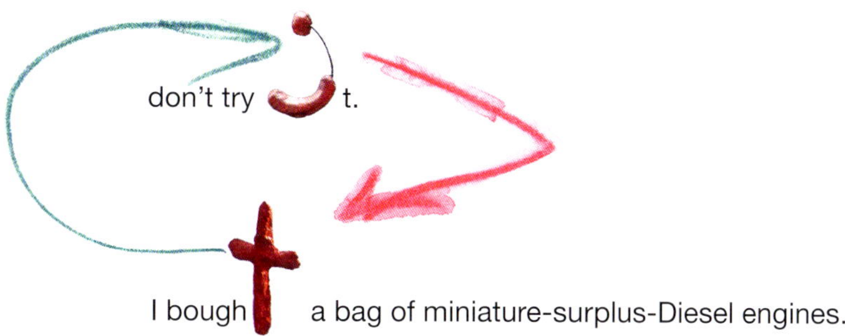

I knew someone on the "college ship."

Get

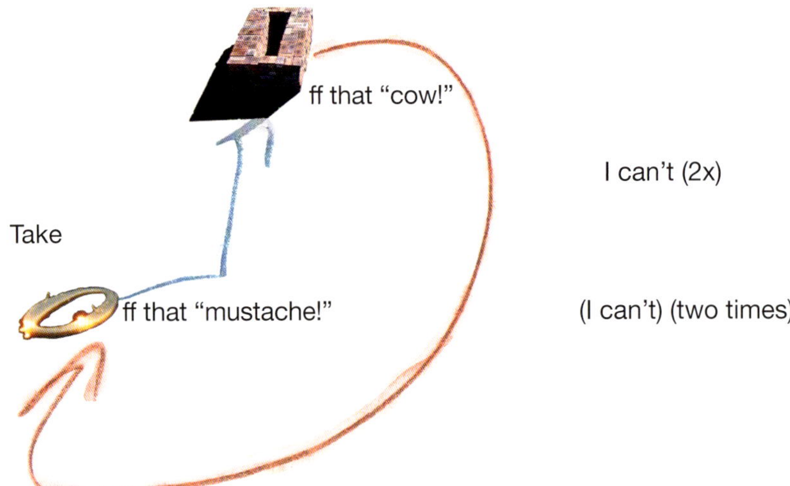

I can't (2x)

Take

ff that "mustache!"

(I can't) (two times)

3

I found a bag of rubber hatchets—

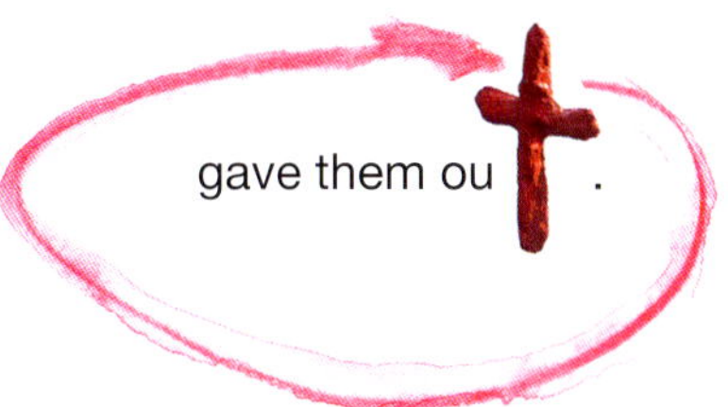

gave them ou .

4

no one chop the

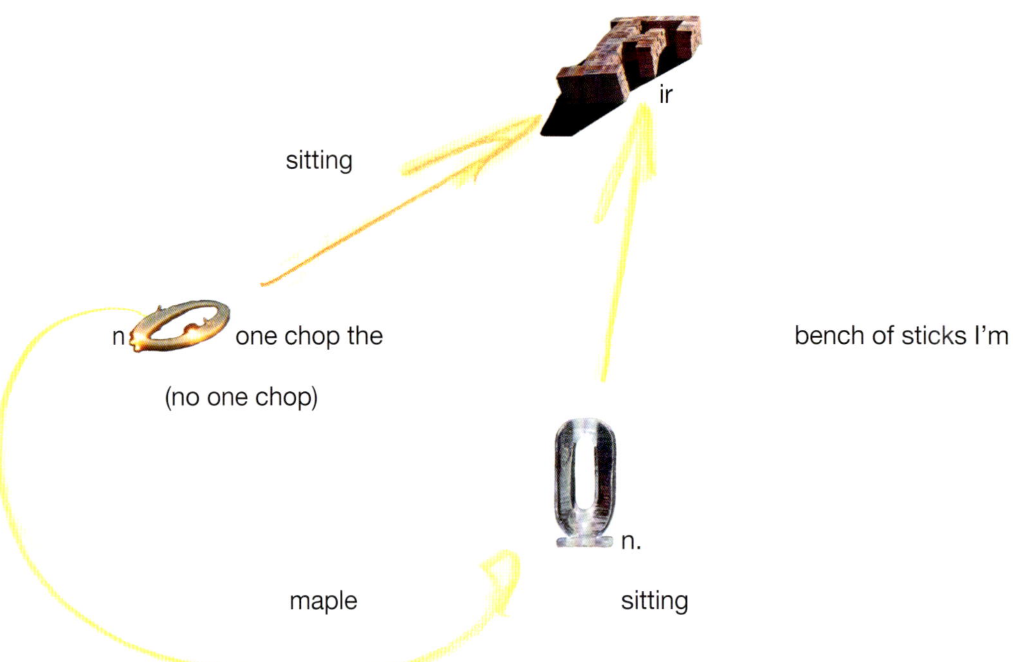

5

two railways

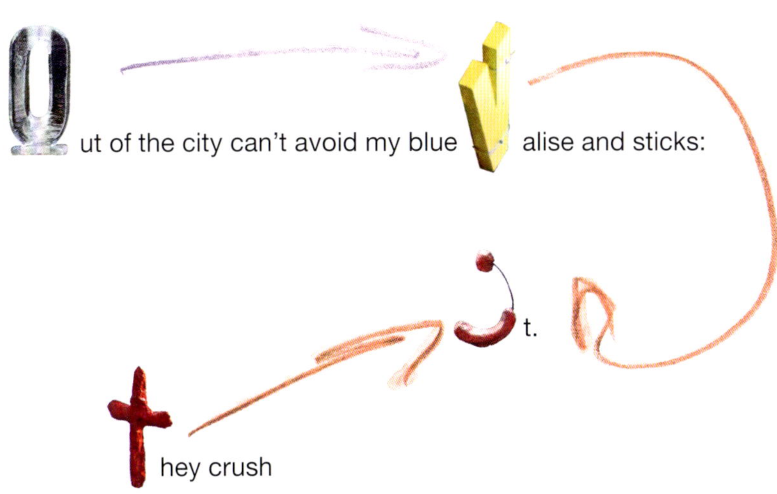

them.

The Beveled Bench and Tube Claire

I 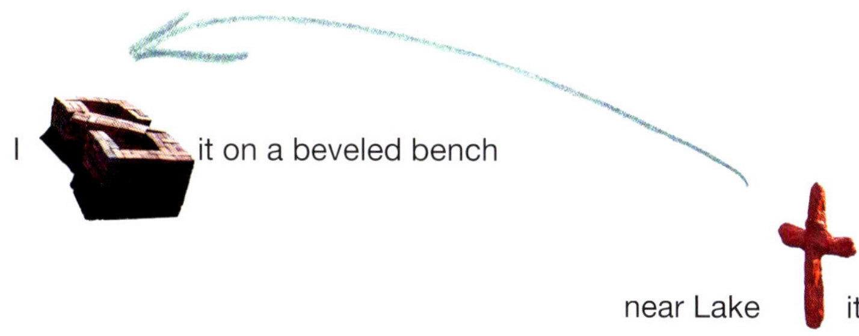 it on a beveled bench

near Lake it.

I like it.

1. _______________________________

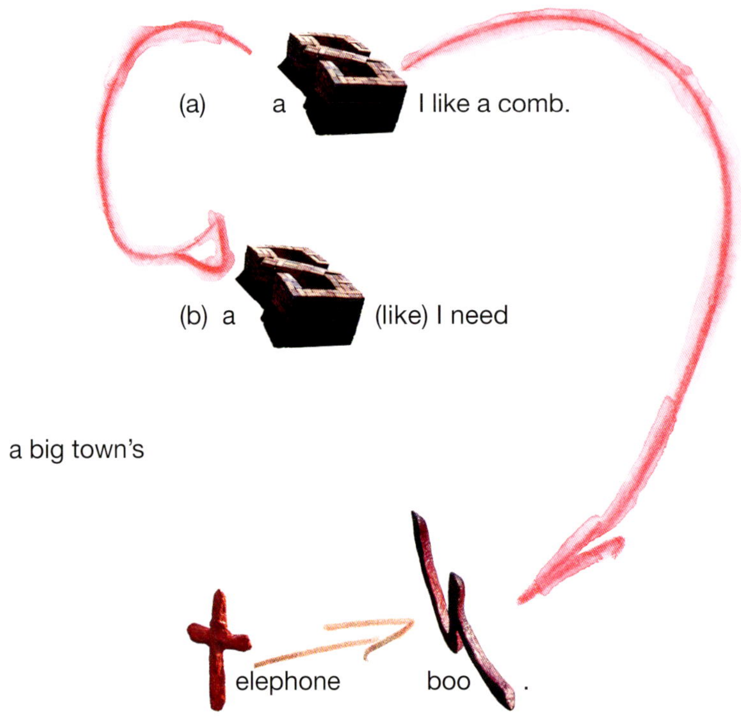
(a)   a   I like a comb.

(b) a   (like) I need

a big town's

elephone   boo   .

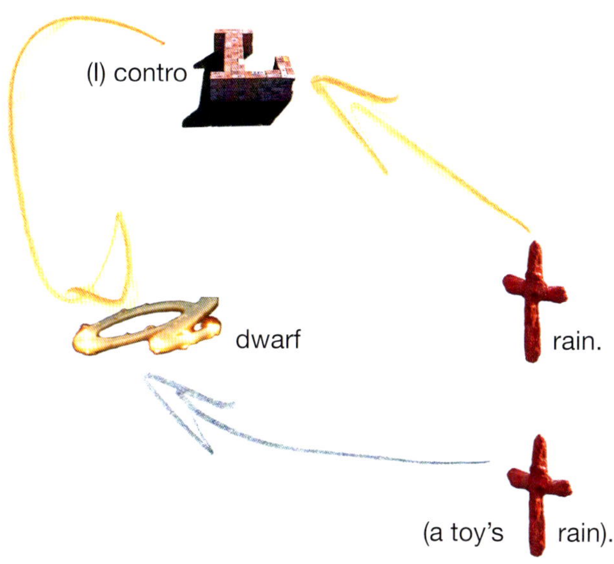
(l) contro
dwarf
rain.
(a toy's   rain).

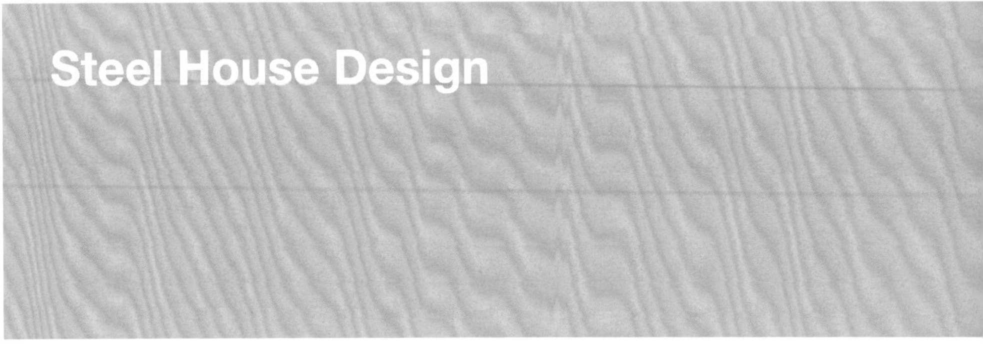

Steel House Design

(On Land) (Bie 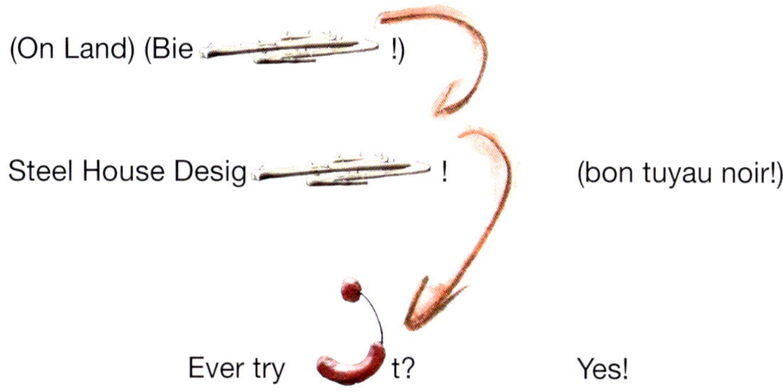 !)

Steel House Desig !   (bon tuyau noir!)

Ever try t?   Yes!

Ha!   Always comes out

         "luxur   bunker!"

Ha!   (unny) usually comes out

"luxury-battleship-captain's quarters!"   (Bie   !)

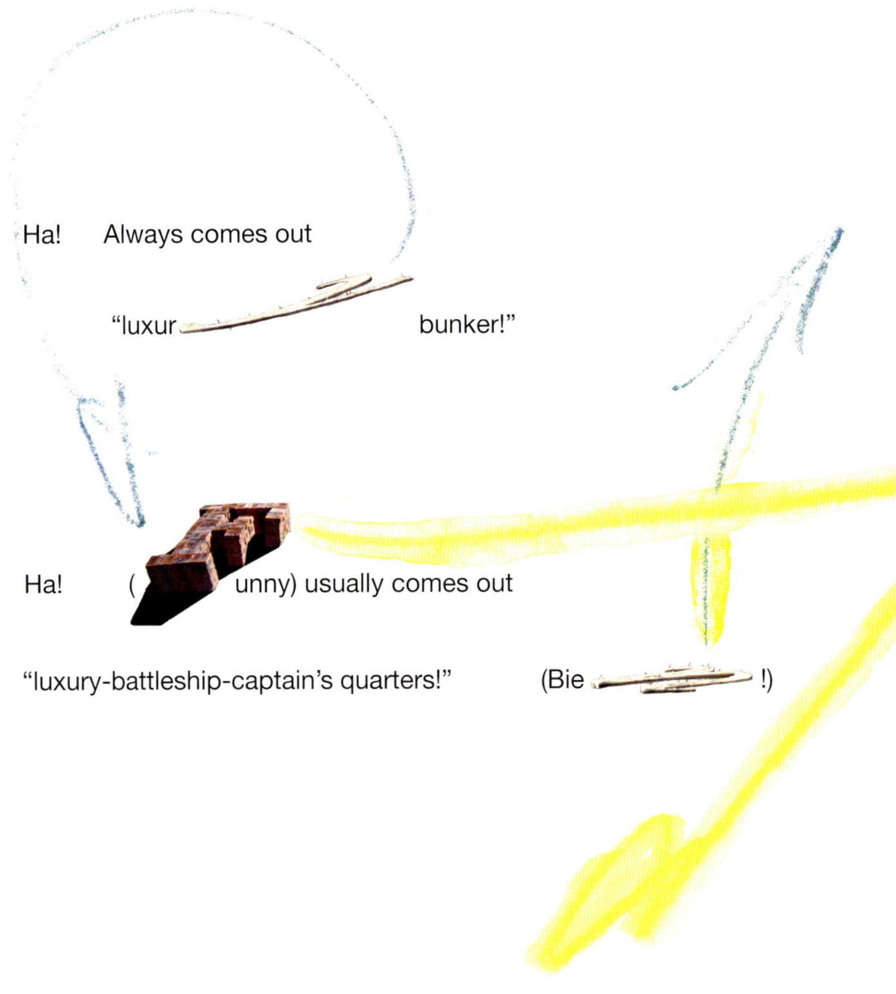

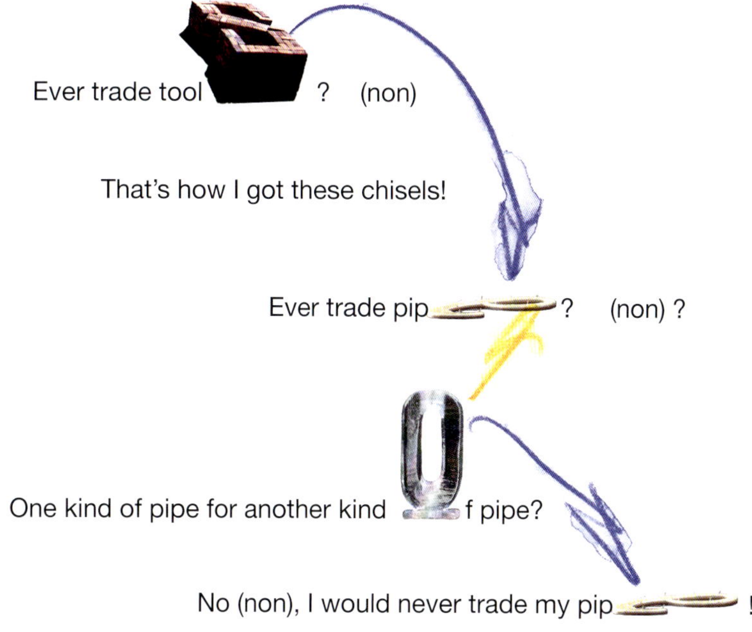

Ever trade tool   ?   (non)

That's how I got these chisels!

Ever trade pip   ?   (non) ?

One kind of pipe for another kind   f pipe?

No (non), I would never trade my pip   !

I tried to di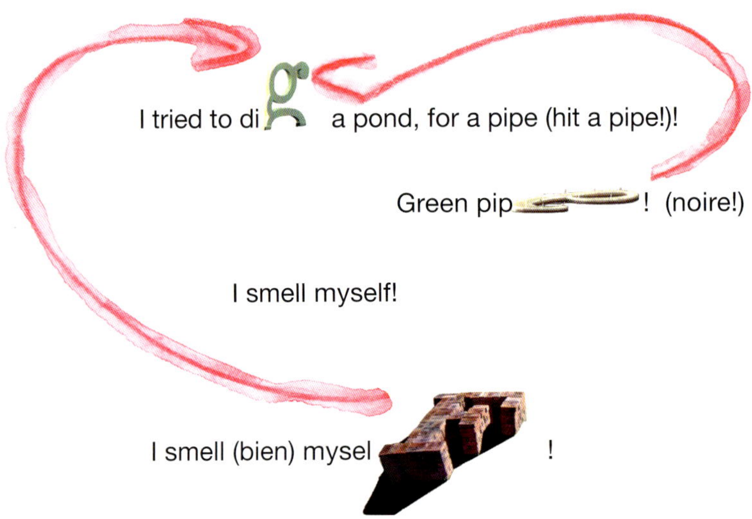 a pond, for a pipe (hit a pipe!)!

Green pip   ! (noire!)

I smell myself!

I smell (bien) mysel   !

4   (At Sea) (Très Bien!)

Hanging on hooks near the "Celebrity" shelf: pipe:

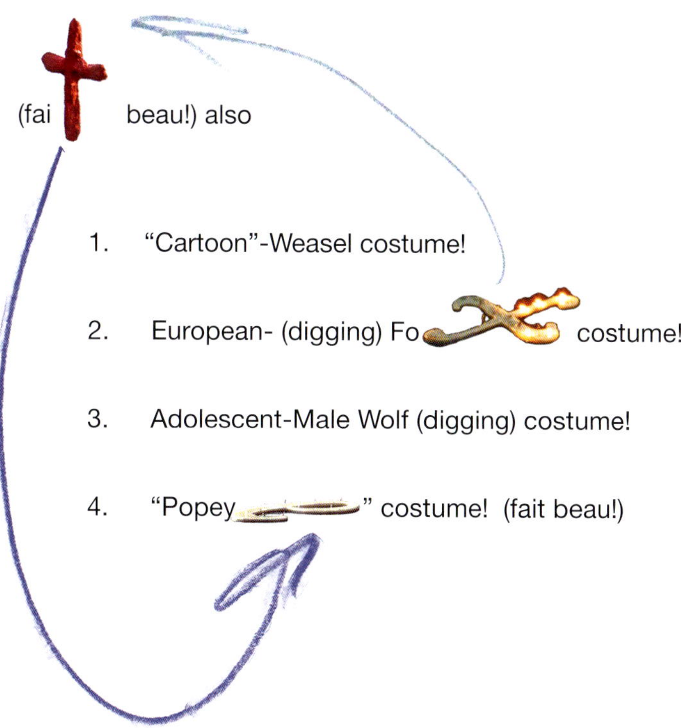

(fai   beau!) also

1.   "Cartoon"-Weasel costume!

2.   European- (digging) Fo   costume!

3.   Adolescent-Male Wolf (digging) costume!

4.   "Popey   " costume! (fait beau!)

5

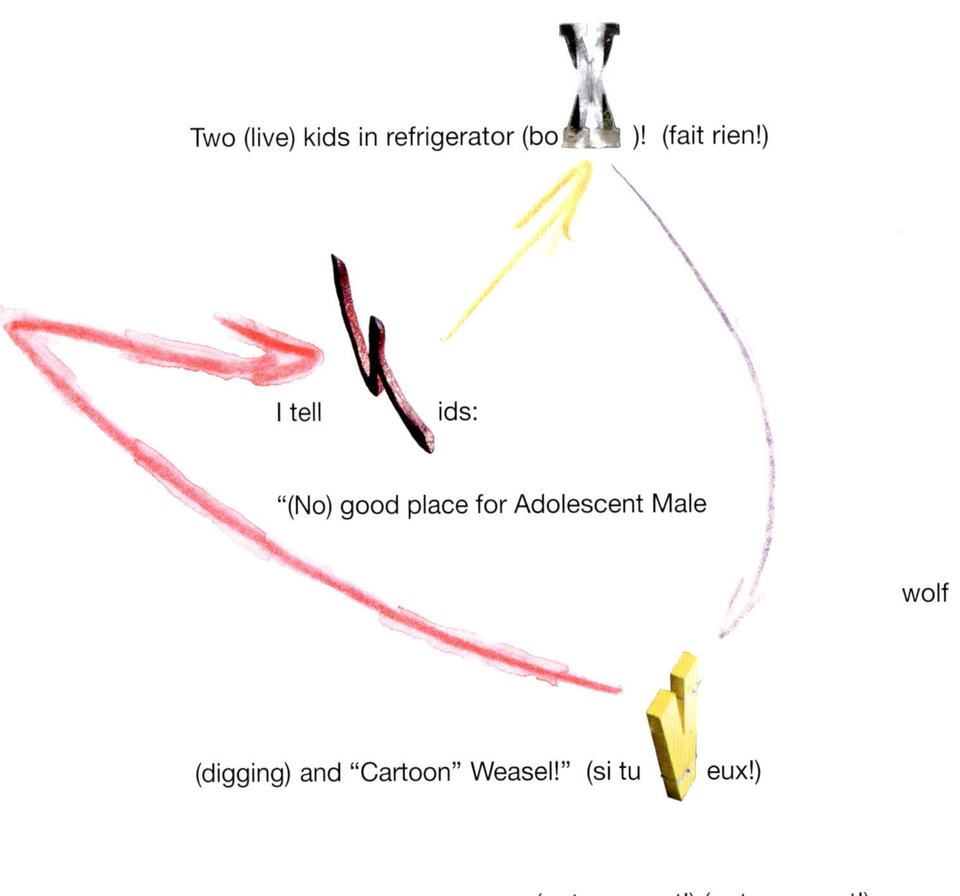

Two (live) kids in refrigerator (bo   )! (fait rien!)
I tell   ids:
"(No) good place for Adolescent Male
wolf
(digging) and "Cartoon" Weasel!" (si tu   eux!)
(not a parent!) (not apparent!)

Mercury

(Hg) (the liquid)

where

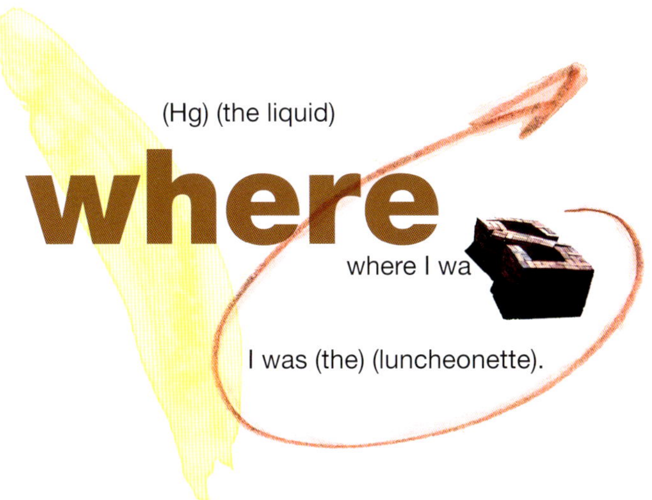

I was (the) (luncheonette).

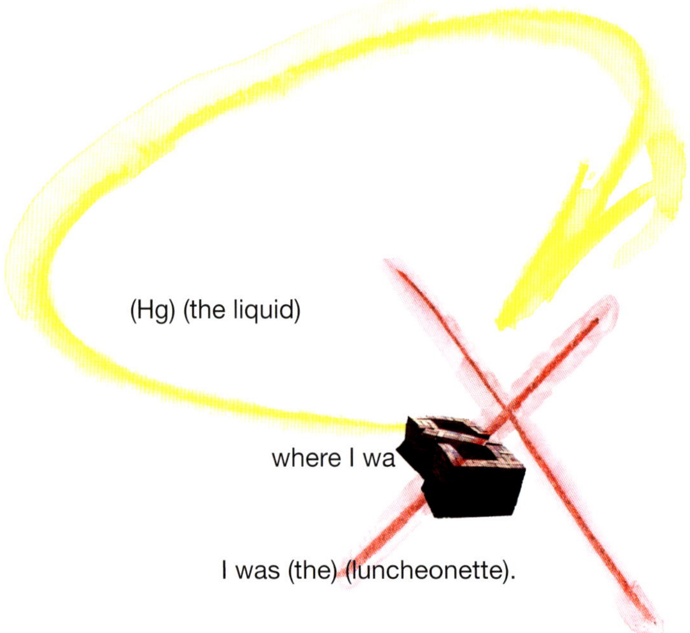

(Hg) (the liquid)
where I wa
I was (the) (luncheonette).

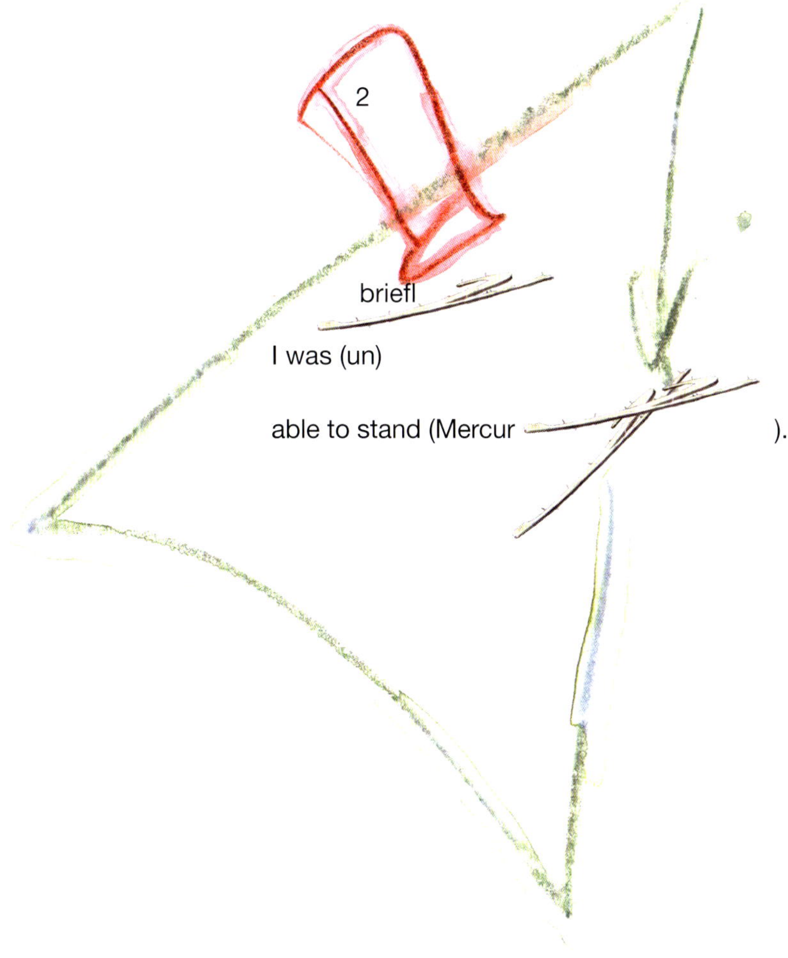

2
briefl
I was (un)
able to stand (Mercur   ).

3

my arm, lion arm

m   head, lion head

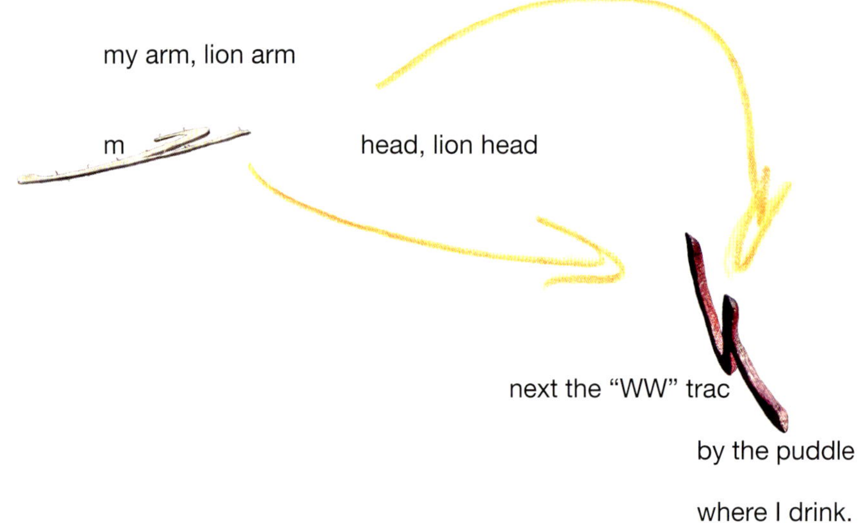

next the "WW" trac

by the puddle

where I drink.

4

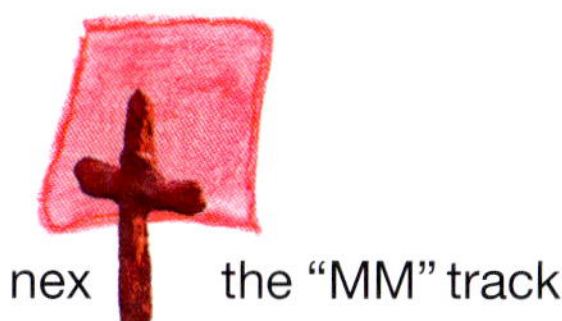

nex the "MM" track

by the puddle

where I drink.

4

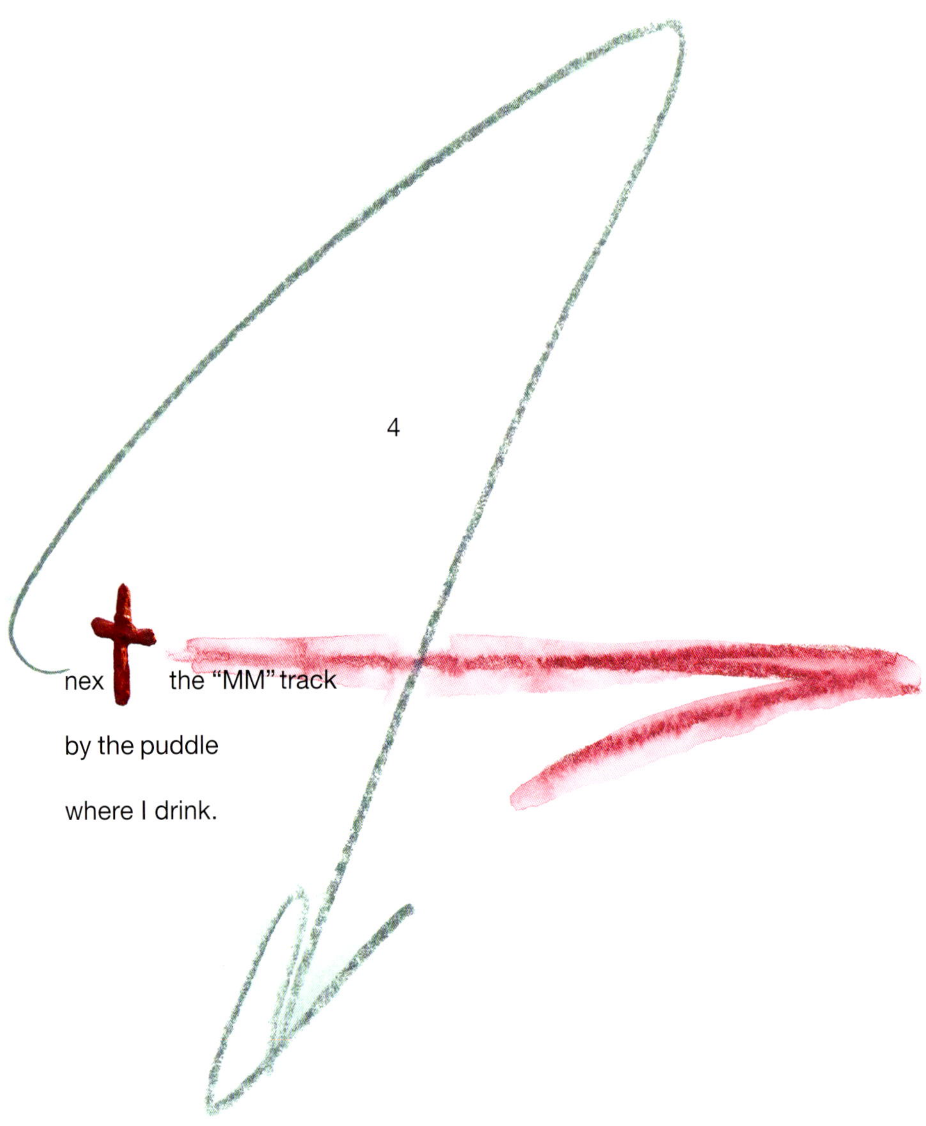

nex the "MM" track

by the puddle

where I drink.

5

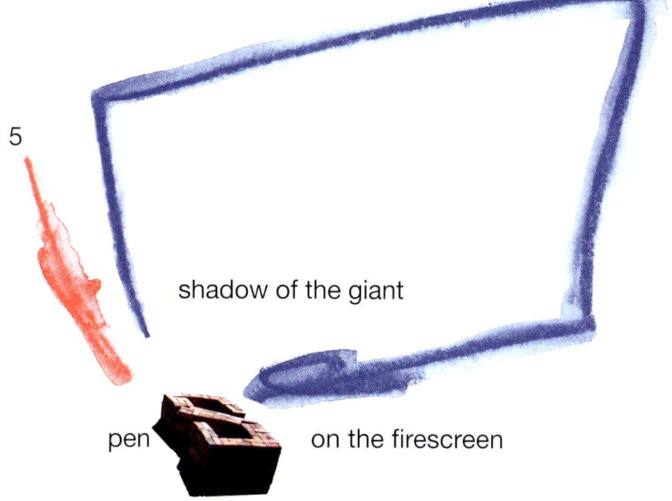

I see the lead (Pb)

did I touch it?

Uncle Jim: A Donkey

They're "pati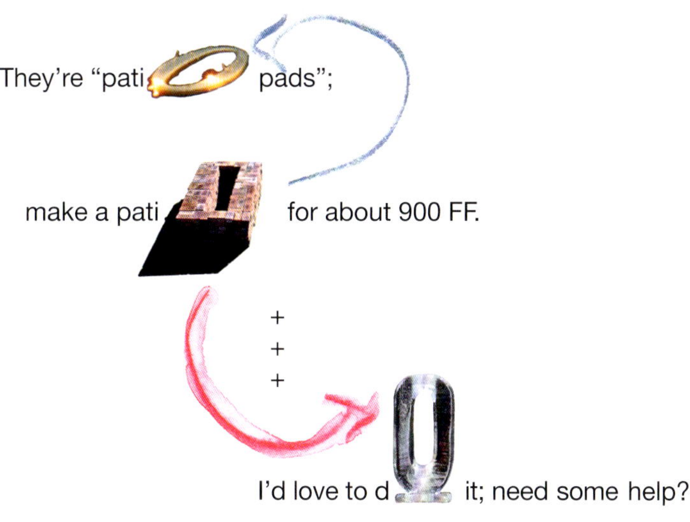 pads";

make a pati for about 900 FF.

+
+
+

I'd love to d it; need some help?

Ask him; ask Jim.

B

What happened to the old donk

"Uncle Jim,"

the "smokey" one?

I ate him

+++++++
+++++++
+++++++
+++++++

                                        +
                                        +
                                        +
                                        +
                                        +
                                        +
                                        +

What happened to the old donk

"Uncle Jim,"

the "smokey" one?

I ate him

C

+++++++
+++++++
+++++++
+++++++

+
+
+
+
+
+
+

+
+
+
+
+
+

There were 20 to 30 radios

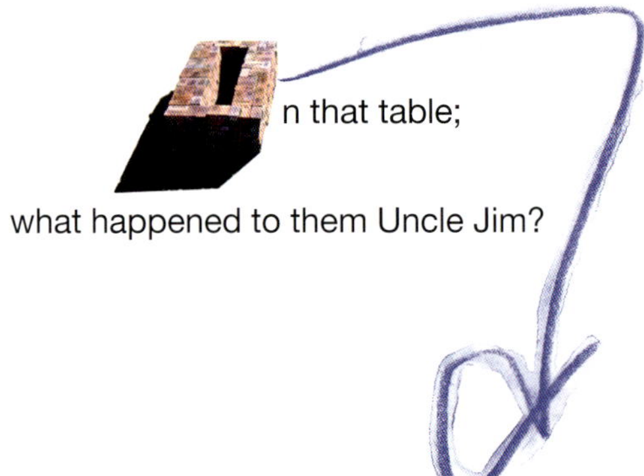

what happened to them Uncle Jim?

D

"Listen (or tune in)

    I was in a cigar-smoking contest

          for over a year and a hal

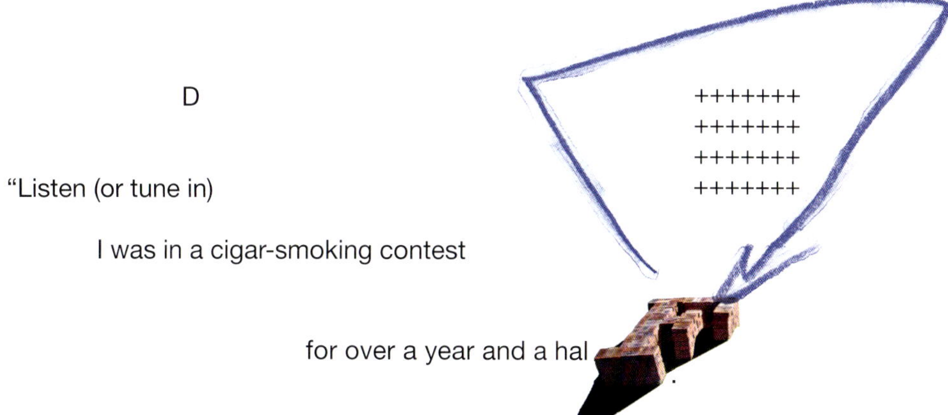

I was lucky enough to win

this radio, pati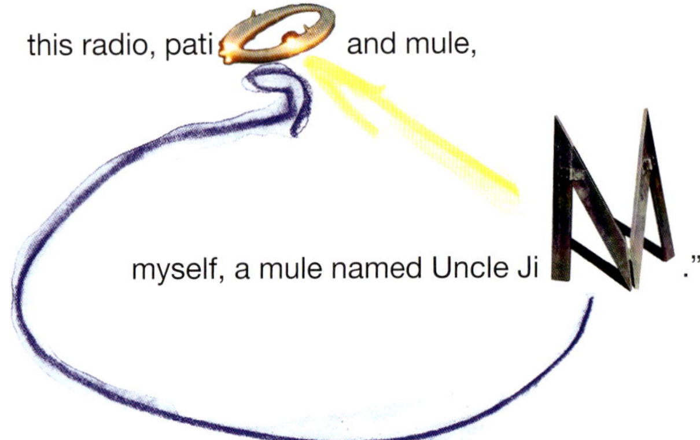 and mule,

myself, a mule named Uncle Ji   ."

Sly Fry

sly

(SI   )

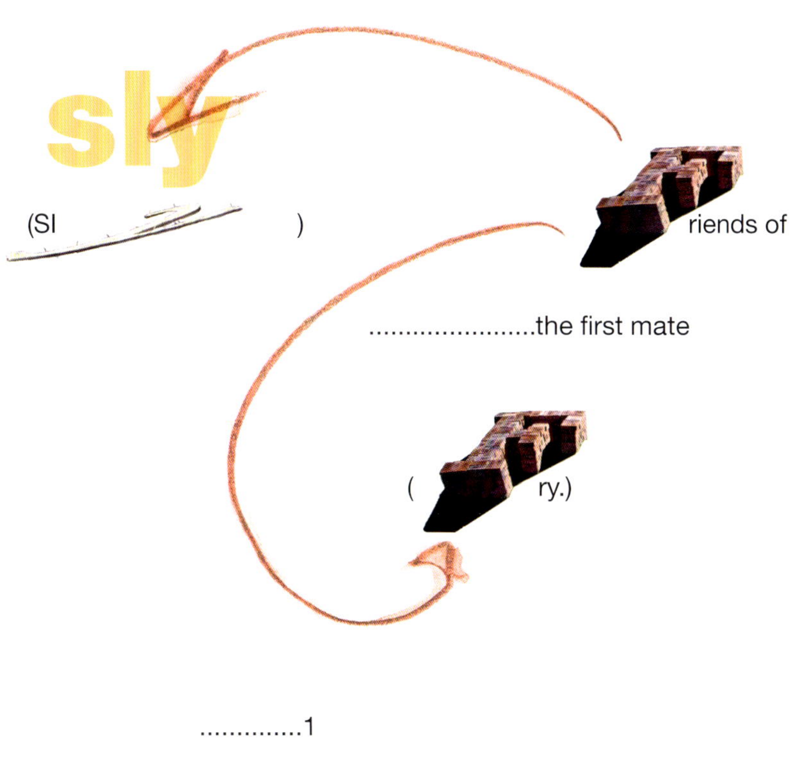
riends of

........................the first mate

(ry.)

..............1

+++++++++
++++++++++++++++++

I stick

Black Squirrel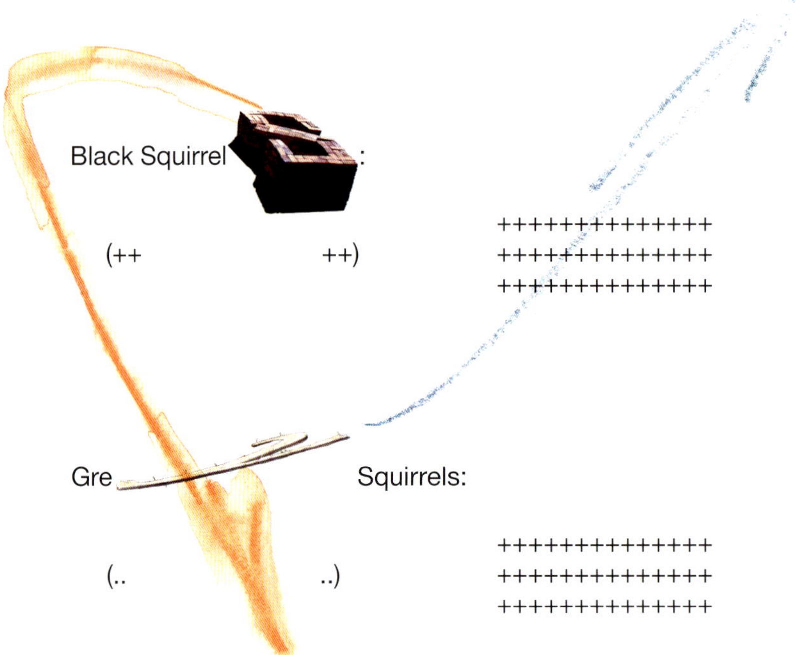 :

(++   ++)   ++++++++++++++
                                         ++++++++++++++
                                         ++++++++++++++

Gre   Squirrels:

                                         ++++++++++++++
(..   ..)   ++++++++++++++
                                         ++++++++++++++

I stick

Black Squirrel 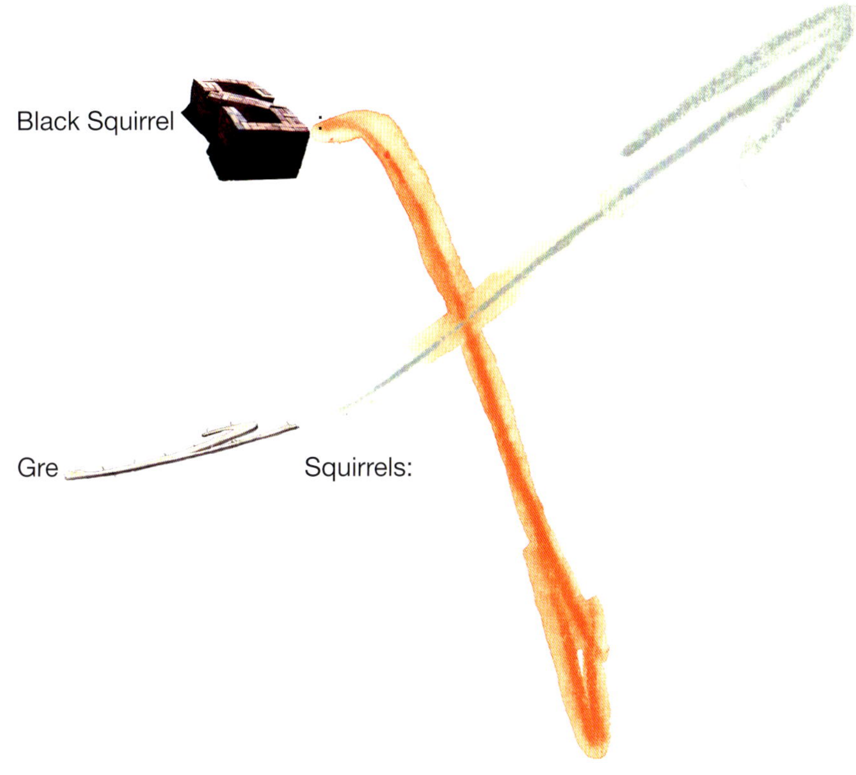

Gre   Squirrels:

2

had a

++++++
++++++

Haddock's

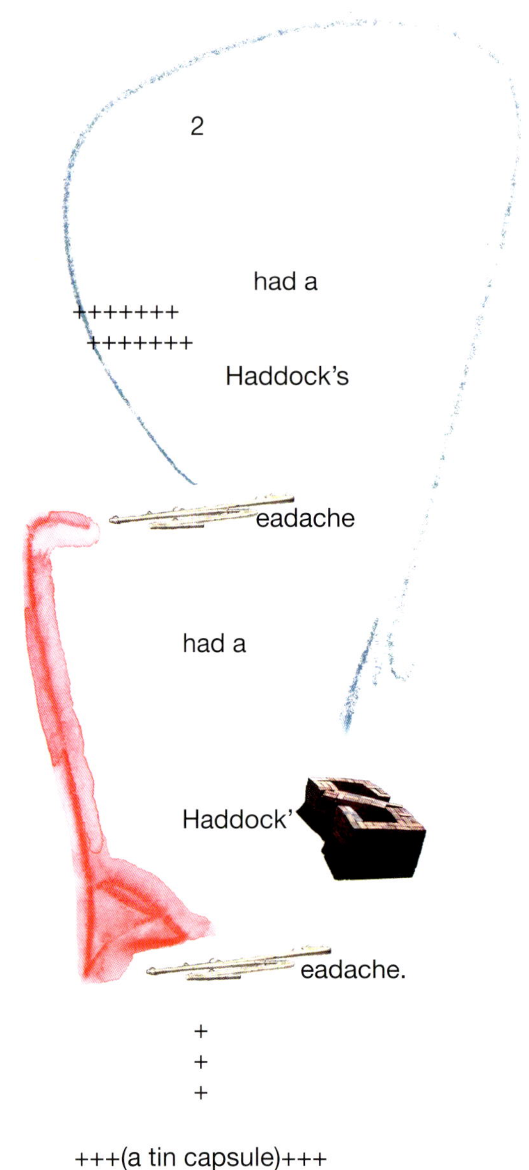

eadache

had a

Haddock'

eadache.

+
+
+

+++(a tin capsule)+++

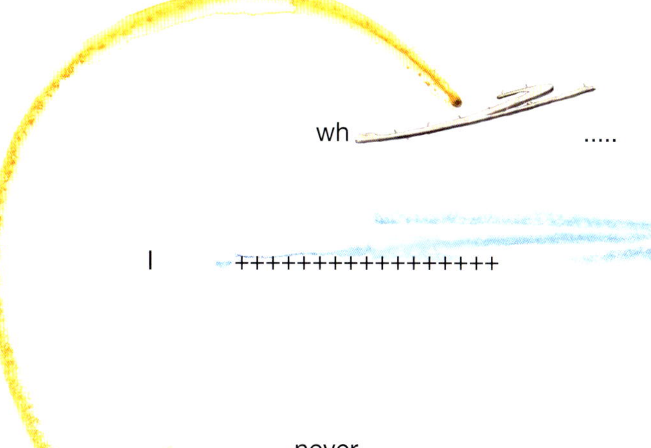

wh   .....

I   +++++++++++++++++

.....................never

a) comb them

b) smudg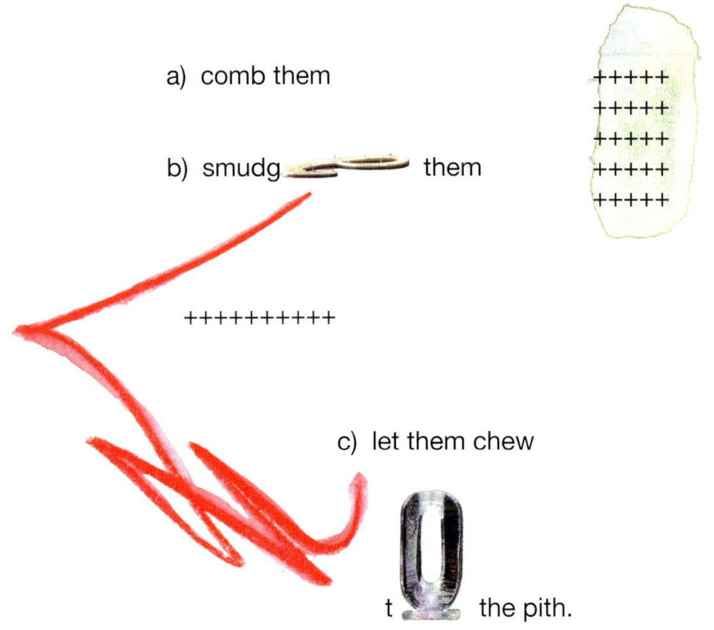 them

+++++
+++++
+++++
+++++
+++++

+++++++++

c) let them chew

t   the pith.

+++++++++++++++
+++++++++++++++ 3

4

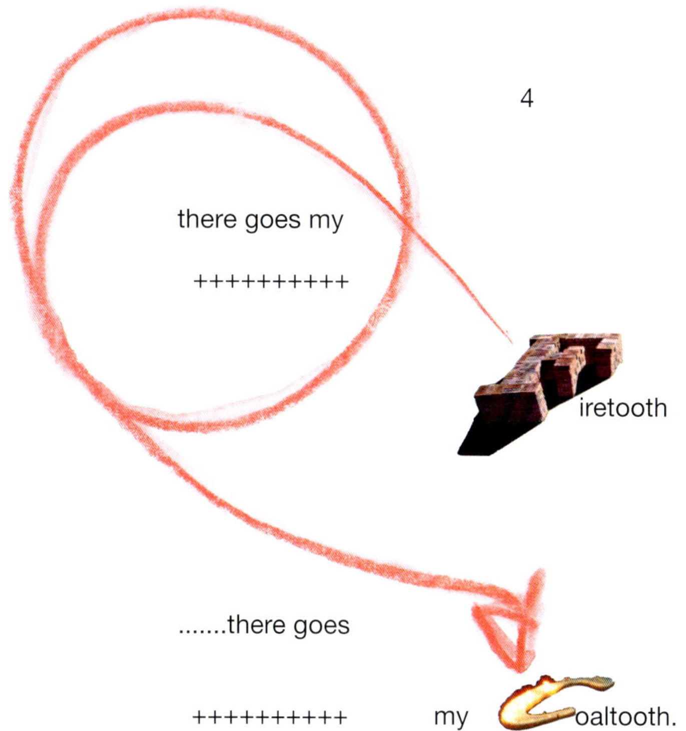

Tee-Pee Cathedral (1988–1991)

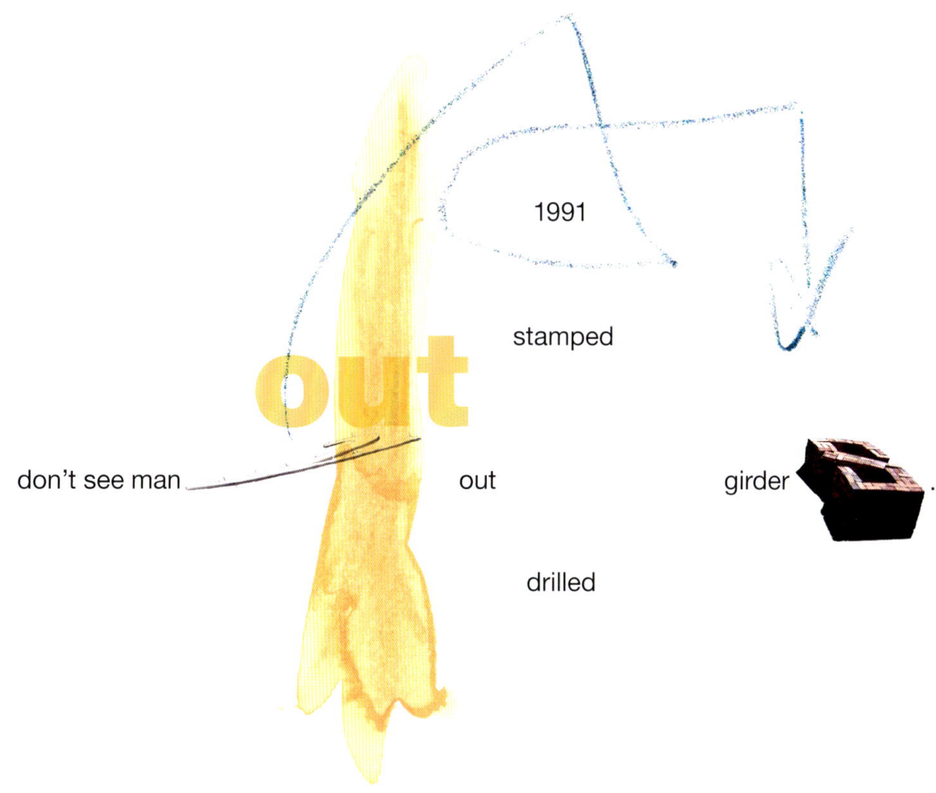
1991

out

stamped

don't see man   out   girder

drilled

can't say to wife:

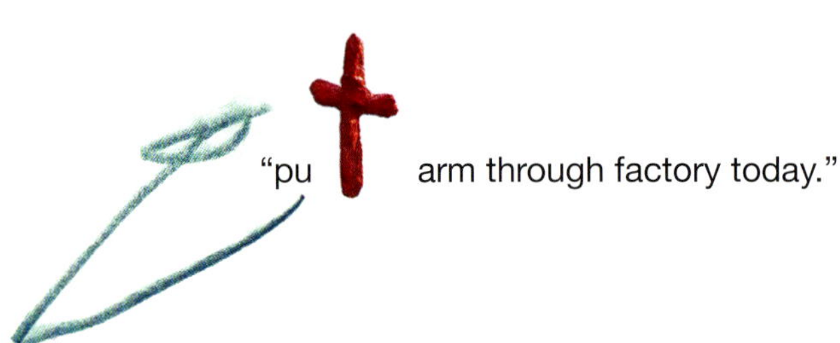

"pu   arm through factory today."

1988

tee-pee

cathedra 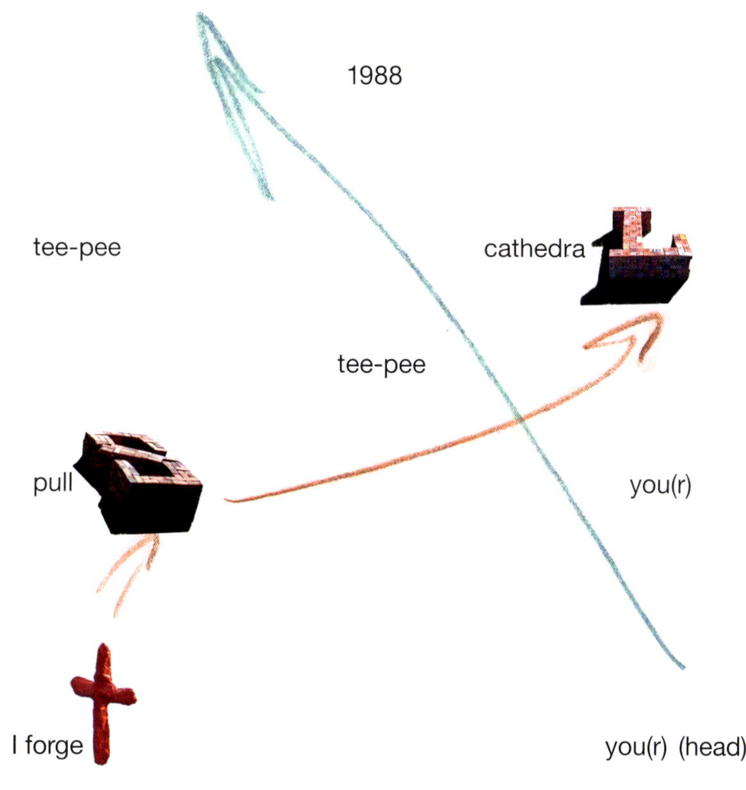

tee-pee

pull

you(r)

I forge

you(r) (head)

(very compelling).

Monkey, Pigeon or Sheep

I 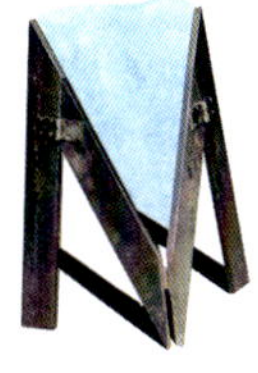onkey, Pigeon or Sheep (animal-material)

II

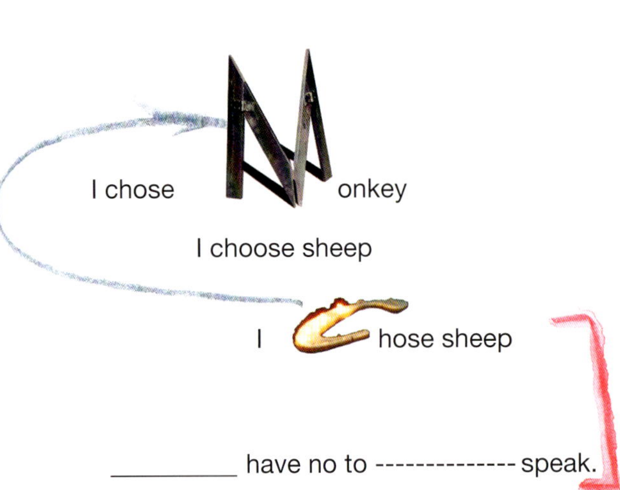

iron

III   (Stock im Eisen)[1]   (Wien)

________ is a boastful material (instant)

rubber (the)

became the plastic (the)

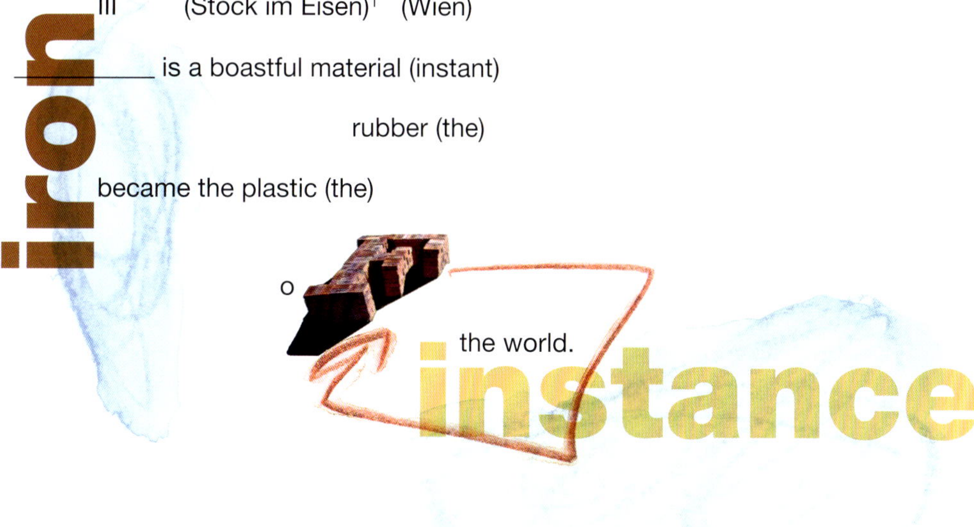

---

[1] The "Stock im Eisen"—a Viennese spruce tree into which journeymen locksmiths drove nails for good luck. A part of the original tree, which dates from the early 16th century, is on display in the Historisches Museum der Stadt Wien.

III   (Stock im Eisen)[2] (Wien)

__________ is a boastful material (instant)

rubber (the)

became the plastic (the)

o 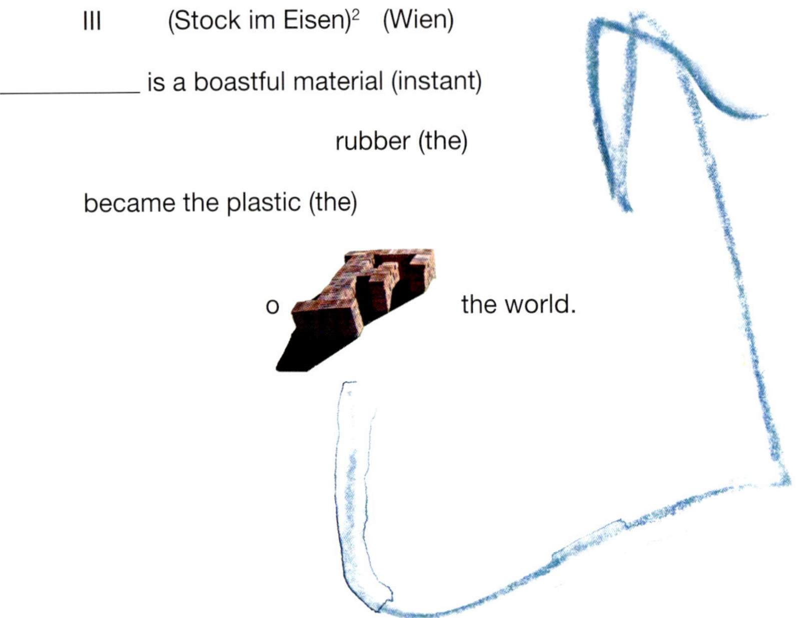 the world.

---

[2] The "Stock im Eisen"—a Viennese spruce tree into which journeymen locksmiths drove nails for good luck. A part of the original tree, which dates from the early 16th century, is on display in the Historisches Museum der Stadt Wien.

IV

Academics (she is an academic: has hand-stamp

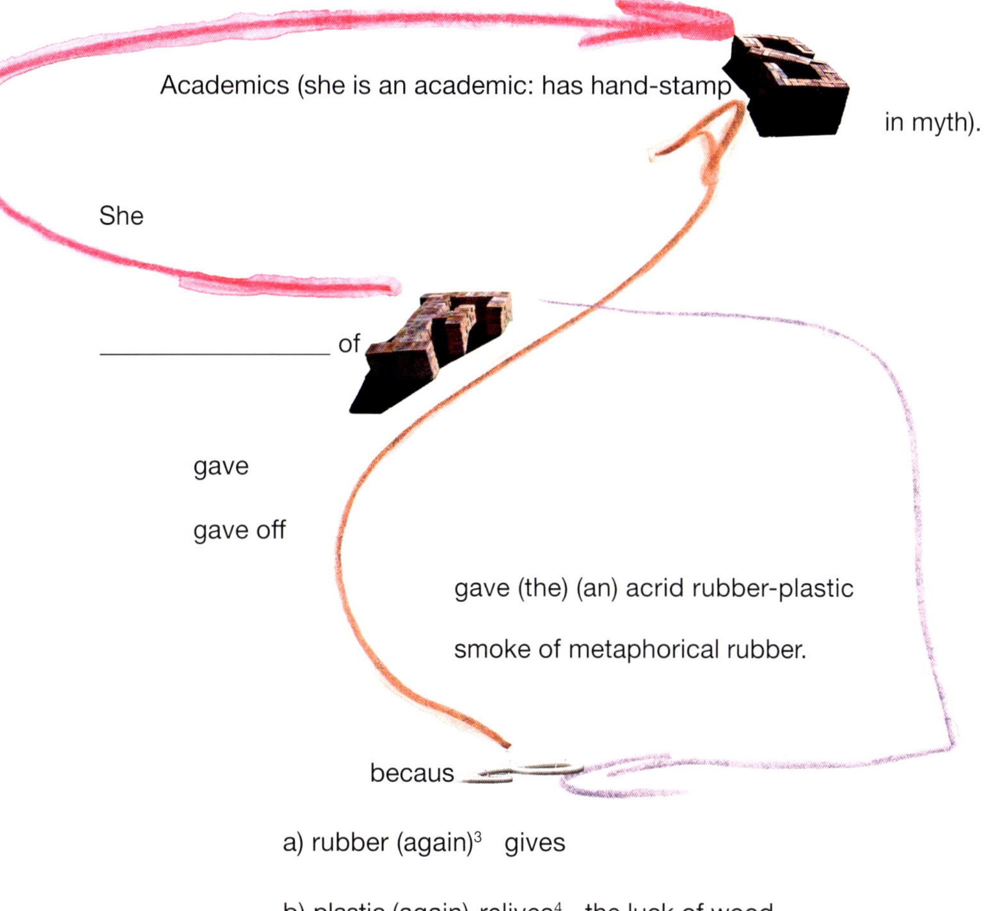

in myth).

She

_________________ of

gave

gave off

gave (the) (an) acrid rubber-plastic

smoke of metaphorical rubber.

becaus

a) rubber (again)[3]   gives

b) plastic (again) relives[4]   the luck of wood.

---

[3] how plastic compares to wood.

[4] also relieves the lucky wood.

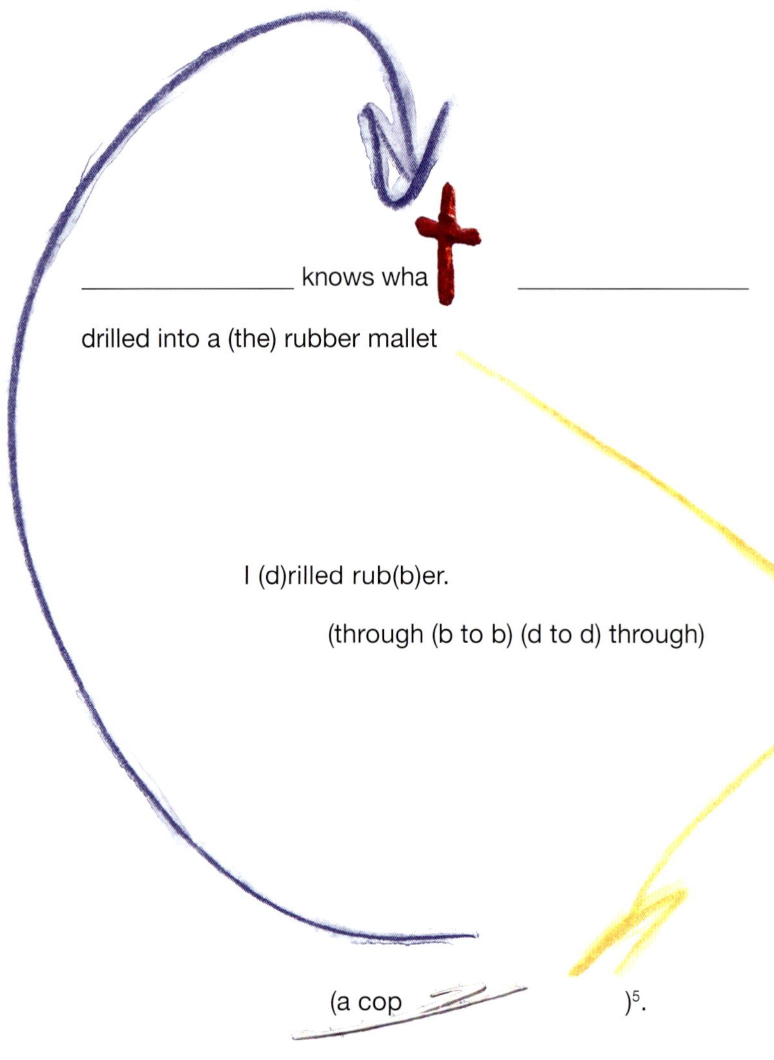

---

[5] a grey, plastic monkey: to fabricate from petrified wood.

VII   Works Cited (temporal and spatial frames)

(1. Large human-spatial [cultural] gaps.)

(2. Large human-temporal gaps.)

"1   No one has tried to find out whether pigeons can sort pictures out by style, so the issue is empirically open. But pigeons are able to sort pictures containing a specific individual person, without being put off by differences in costume or context. Monkeys have no problem identifying pictures of individual monkeys, or, for that matter, individual humans, and will respond with erect hair and scream at a leader showing anger" (Danto 210).

Works Cited

Calinescu, Matei. *Rereading*. New Haven: Yale University Press, 1993.

Danto, Arthur C. "Description and the Phenomenology of Perception." *Visual Theory: Painting and Interpretation*, edited by Norman Bryson, Michael Ann Holly and Keith Moxey. New York: HarperCollins, 1991. 201–215.

Derrida, Jacques. *Writing and Difference*, trans. Alan Bass. Chicago: University of Chicago Press, 1978.

Meehan, Aidan. *Celtic Design: Illuminated Letters*. New York: Thames & Hudson, 1992.

Morris, Charles. *Signs, Language and Behavior*. New York: Pentice-Hall, 1946.

Peirce, Charles Sanders. *The Collected Papers of Charles Sanders Peirce*, edited by Charles Hartshorne and Paul Weiss. Cambridge: Belknap Press of Harvard University Press, 1931–1958.

More titles from 1913 Press:

Dreaming of Ramadi in Detroit, Aisha Sabatini Sloan (2017)
A Turkish Dictionary, Andrew Wessels (2017)
Gray Market, Krystal Languell (2016)
Arcane Rituals from the Future, Leif Haven (2016, selected by Claudia Rankine)
I, Too, Dislike It, Mia You (2016, Editrice's Pick)
Unlikely Conditions, Cynthia Arrieu-King & Hillary Gravendyk (2016)
Abra, Amaranth Borsuk & Kate Durbin (2016)
Pomme & Granite, Sarah Riggs (2015)
Untimely Death is Driven Out Beyond the Horizon, Brenda Iijima (2015)
Full Moon Hawk Application, CA Conrad (Assless Chaps, 2014)
Big House/Disclosure, Mendi & Keith Obadike (2014)
Four Electric Ghosts, Mendi & Keith Obadike (2014)
O Human Microphone, Scott McFarland (2014, selected by Rae Armantrout)
Kala Pani, Monica Mody (2013)
Bravura Cool, Jane Lewty (2012, selected by Fanny Howe)
The Transfer Tree, Karena Youtz (2012)
Conversities, Dan Beachy-Quick & Srikanth Reddy (2012)
Home/Birth: A Poemic, Arielle Greenberg & Rachel Zucker (2011)
Wonderbender, Diane Wald (2011)
Ozalid, Biswamit Dwibedy (2010)
Sightings, Shin Yu Pai (2007)
Seismosis, John Keene & Christopher Stackhouse (2006)
Read 1–6, an annual anthology of inter-translation, Sarah Riggs &
    Cole Swensen, eds.
1913 a journal of forms, Issues 1–6, Sandra Doller, ed.

1913 titles are distributed solely by Small Press Distribution **www.spdbooks.org**.